Another Parenting Book You Don't Need

Jennifer De Paz

XO

Another Parenting Book You Don't Need

With a Side of Unsolicited Advice

Jennifer De Paz

ISBN-13: 978-0-692-19831-5
ISBN-10: 0-692-19831-8

Cover design by Taherul Islam

First Printing

Contents

Sincere Dedications

I dedicate this book, first and foremost, to the real superheroes of this earth: Mothers, yours and mine. Allow me to raise my mug of chamomile tea to the Wombs of Steel!

Natural birth moms, C-section moms, moms of babies born at home, moms of babies born in hospitals, I-Didn't-Know-I-Was-Pregnant moms, breastfeeding moms, bottle-feeding moms, formula-feeding moms, moms whose kids eat Cheetos from between the car seats, moms of multiples, expecting moms, Angel Baby moms, young moms who are growing up with their kids, married moms and single moms who have to work two or more jobs to make ends meet, moms who run their own business, moms who live in leggings and top buns, moms who separated their families to give a better life to their kids, moms who ditched their dreams for a bit to be present, moms working hard on theirs, moms who have had to wait for the kids to go to sleep so they could have a good cry, moms who have gone out looking like complete zombies while the kids look like Gap runway models, stay-at-home moms who don't even know who they are anymore, moms who have a bin somewhere of missing socks because they are determined their counterpart will turn up, moms who own dry shampoo, widowed moms, moms who solve everything with a Magic Eraser, moms who have dropped things in a store to be able to get things for the kids instead, moms who have been moms to other kids who needed them, teachers who are often like moms, moms who swore to never again have another baby but then had more anyway, moms who have gotten the stink eye while yelling at their kids in public, moms who have driven their kids to school braless praying, "I hope this is not the day I get pulled over or get in a fender bender," moms who also have to be dads, moms who carry some sort of mom guilt, moms who never stop giving, never stop believing, and never stop being grateful for the privilege it is to be called "MOMMOMMOMMOMMOMMOMMOMMOM-MOMMOMMOMMOMMOMMOM!"

I dedicate this book to my parents who traumatized me just the right amount to not cause any permanent damage. Their tough and often military-like upbringing provided me with a strong backbone. Nowadays, their words reverberate inside my skull and I know for certain that it is because of them that I have this very necessary sense of humor. This combination of strength and lightheartedness has come in rather handy now that I am raising kids of my own. Although I still don't really know what I am doing exactly, I am hoping to be half as amazing as they are because, let's face it, they are still raising me, and my mother still makes me feel like she will ground me at any moment if I leave my house without a sweater.

I dedicate this compilation of earnest nonsense to my kids who probably won't find this amusing until they have children of their own. It is their little faces I seek for motivation and strength. It is those same faces I must turn and hide from as I eat candy bars behind their backs when they bring forth the mass of mayhem.

This book could not have happened without the support of the appointed nanny, my fiancé. He allowed the kids to destroy the house at times when I had to step out to focus and meditate. A lot of laundry went undone, and some days they all had to eat cat food so you guys could have this parenting book on your coffee table. Actually, I hope you hide it.

Last, but actually first, I would give almost anything to place this book on my grandmother's lap and hear her say her magic words, "I am so glad you are happy." I felt her love and guidance throughout this entire project. She, who was a constant in my life, always cheering me up and encouraging me to do what makes me happiest, is what inspired me the most. I'll tell her all about it when I see her in my dreams and I'll apologize to her for using profanity to get my points across.

Introduction

No one has the heart to tell you the truth about parenting. I think it all revolves around different types of fears. What will people think if I admit this is no stroll through a well-lit park? Hell, it's more like a walk through a category 5 hurricane with a tornado chasing you while you're wearing heels and holding ten grocery bags.

It could be they are afraid of hearing their own voice cry out in truth, pain, and submissiveness. Personally, I think the guilt of admitting that becoming a parent is pretty listless would be an emotional burden. Hence, all the lies, and double hence, the discrepancies of what it really means to have kids. Who really discloses all the highly coveted pleasures you'll actually be giving up, like a peaceful thirty minutes in the bathroom? No one.

So, here I am to offer you some crude advice throughout this book. If you find yourself at a crossroad between confused and offended, perhaps I succeeded, in which case I encourage you to use this book as a coaster. Evidently, you have lost your sense of humor and I blame the kids. Much like other parenting books, this one is a combination of another stranger's opinions and experiences, which hold zero bearing on what you will actually do as a parent after reading it. Derived from my nine years of parenting, that feel more like ninety, I have chosen to submerge you deep into various parenting topics, many of which are frequently avoided. I know people don't care for unsolicited advice, but trust me that you will always receive it. I, myself, have been a giver as well as the recipient. I have learned that people, more often than not, prefer to continue doing things their own way or even the way their families have done it for generations, regardless if there is a better, smarter, or safer way. This seems to be true in almost all life situations but rings truest when it comes to raising kids.

If this book seems biased to mothers, know that it was executed this way on purpose. I took into consideration that nine out of ten men don't read instruction manuals, much less a parenting book. That's not to discount the many fathers whose efforts are not subpar, because I know amazing fathers exist. Still, until they can find items around the house without asking their spouse, learn to braid hair, throw out empty containers instead of putting them back, and keep track of all birthdays and special events, they don't get a chapter in my book. The fact that I even mention the word "father" ought to be of ample appreciation, so, in my Andre 3000 voice, "This one right here goes out to all the baby's mamas, mama's mamas, baby mama's mamas...."

Chapter 1
Debunking Parenting Ideals

I strongly believe there isn't a parenting book in this vast universe that is going to guide us on the righteous path to raising incredible kids. What I am sure about, on plenty of levels, is that we need each other. Mothers need other mothers, and fathers need to remember where to put the keys after they use the car. We are each in our unique but beautiful and chaotic storm. We're going to get through it, in 18–25 years, because we have no choice, but we do have wine and chocolate.

Why Moms Are the Way They Are

Remember how upset your mother always was when you were growing up? I do. Everyone's mom was that way, and if she wasn't, then she was having several cocktails a day. Bunch of mad old ladies, always yelling about something, bringing down the mojo of the whole house, right? I get it now. I understand why such misery. Now, I am that lady! I made it! We're "that way" because life is gravy until you reproduce and now every time you're about to smile, someone drops a cup of something on your freshly mopped floor or you open the mailbox and there are five bills and invitations to kids' birthday parties you'd really rather not go to.

Each time you're about to exhale, someone is crying because another someone is being mean to them and you have to pretend to care or you're being asked where the contact solution is, being that it is allocated in the same place every day. You might be enjoying a smoothie in an empty kitchen, and you have to put it down to put a Band-Aid on a scratch.

Moms' forlorn expressions come from having to change their tampon with three people staring at them, having to drink cold coffee that wasn't meant to be cold, and having to put off things of their own to put everyone else first.

At the very least, nowadays, mothers can file empty complaints on a social media platform, hide in the garage to meander back and forth with other miserable moms, and send each other virtual hugs. Our moms didn't have any of that. They had to deal with our crappy attitudes and their boring lives alone in their houses, counting down the days when everyone would move the hell out. And dads—they are just tired of having to hear us complain about all of this. Mom, if you are reading this, I see it all so clearly now. I deserved all the shoes you threw my way. One thing I find complete solace in is that all of these aggravations are worth the incredible comfort I feel in knowing that because I have children, I am never alone in the world.

Prior to becoming a mother, I often heard magical and endearing tales of the thrilling ride that is parenthood. I dare say, the vast majority of these stories were highly embellished, and come to think of it, expressed ever so enthusiastically so that misery can provoke more company.

> *Come over to the dark side so we can discuss wipe warmers and breast pumps on Friday night because it's life-changing! There's nothing quite like waking up seven times a night to get vomited on! Come hither! It's a dream, I tell ya!*

I am now aware that all parents are walking around with half a soul because kids suck the soul right out of your ass. Next time you see footage of a baby's first birthday party, zoom in on the parents' faces. They have no souls. They were ripped out by that adorable baby. They're tired beyond recognition. They are basically celebrating that they survived the first year.

You probably won't hear things like, "It actually gets harder" or "The first twenty years are the hardest." No one is going to tell you that you will begin to age rapidly from the second you eject the baby from your body. You aren't warned that from here on out, the years are going to fly by you as if you were in some sort of fast-forwarding time machine. Research shows you will age double on each birthday for every kid you have. All research pertaining to this was done by me. Kids evaporate your collagen, rip your dreams to shreds, and always find time to step on your big toe. They are like little connoisseurs of parenthood patience and how to exasperate it. Yet, despite all the tribulations of being a parent, it is almost a paranormal phenomenon how the face of a mother or father seems to light up whenever they are talking about their snotty-nosed brat(s). Those kids could be Satan's spawn, but if you listen to parents talk about their kids, it is a beautiful thing. Their eyes glisten, and you can almost feel their hearts jumping out of their chests. That could also be anxiety, but we can deem it complete and utter obsession and adoration.

Luckily for you, I'm here to spill the parenting beans and tell you the cold hard truth: parenting is nothing more than an immense inconvenience, one with zero monetary compensation, and more often than not, you will almost have to beg for a simple thank you.

You will begin to sense that being underappreciated is normal in your life now. I would go as far as to say that your emotions and well-being will come last, too, until you begin to fight for your place in the family totem pole. At the same time, something with as much simplicity as a scribbled drawing on a piece of paper or a tight hug from tiny arms will rejuvenate you. Like a phoenix, you will rise again from your ashes, reaffirmed that the unparalleled love you possess for your children is not in vain. It's a total contortion of the cranium. That's a fancy way of saying 'mind fuck' in a parenting book.

Mom Qualifications

While some moments you will be flying high, with inexplicable joy that cannot be superseded by anything under the sun, a great deal of your life as a parent will be spent asking "Why?" into the universe. Many people will tell you that becoming a mother or father will fulfill you and make you the happiest you have ever been. I will ungracefully debunk that myth, too. That isn't what kids come into the world to do! It's quite the opposite, as a matter of fact. First, you must ask yourself the magic question, "Am I happy now?" Are you someone whose happiness is dependent on a preexisting or futuristic definition of happiness? I can assure you that having kids will add many joyous bonuses to your life, but it will also cause you anxiety, crow's feet, indigestion, high blood pressure, nausea, fatigue, and even loneliness. Any of the side effects of prescribed medication can also ring true for parenting.

Do not birth children because you hope to fill a void in your life or because you want to breed a best friend. Let me tell you that no matter how many matching outfits you have with your mini-me, this is not the epitome of happiness. I guarantee you there will be moments when you want to field-goal-kick your "mini you" across the living room. Ever so slowly, you'll realize how much your child reminds you of someone you know. It's you! They will pick up your sarcasm and your quirks. It's almost inevitable. The more like you they become, the more irritated you'll spend your days, wondering if it's all a cruel joke. Yes, it is. Karma doesn't lose an address, let's say.

I hate to be the bearer of bad (and obvious) news, but this is an upside-down world we are living in, where things seem to worsen by the day. It's tough on parents who wish to shield their kids from the perverse, unfair, and hideous truths we cannot escape. Truthfully, it is with the most brazen of attitudes that people choose to procreate at all. The thought of being able to shove these kids right back up where they came from, for their own good, doesn't seem too terrible. We don't have that option.

I am qualified to disclose this plethora of truths and advice because I have been several types of mothers at this point, except a married one. I was in a relationship with the father of my oldest daughter, which was basically a marriage but not a harmonious one. It lasted until she was a little over a year old. I have been a working mom for Corporate America, working nine-hour days and leaving my baby with a babysitter. I have been a single mom with a toddler, with little to no help from her father. I have been a self-employed mother working from home. Currently, I am a stay-at-home mom with two little girls, engaged to the love of my life, sharing with you the real and raw triumphs and stipulations that is parenthood. I dare say I am overqualified. I've been frowning for nine years, so the line between my eyebrows, the glabella, got pretty deep. Thank goodness for Botox, which keeps me looking radiant while I remain pissed. I have also been laughing incredulously because, damn, kids are funny! I also can't cough, sneeze, laugh too hard, or jump without peeing because of two natural births. I don't know how many times I left a Zumba class like a bat out of hell to use the bathroom. It's not the least bit cute. All of this lack of sex appeal also adds to my resume of Motherhood Qualifications. More than your sanity, you will long for your tight vagina.

If you saw me in action with my children or looked at the collection of photographs I keep of us, you would gather that motherhood is something I always wanted. You'd think I was the kind of girl who couldn't wait to grow up and have kids and who dreamed of the day I would become a mother. I was not. I had my moments, though, in my late teens when I would mention the possibility of kids once I was much, much older. That all changed in my twenties. Surprisingly, whether I wanted to be a mother was up to The Universe! It showed me that it was exactly what I was meant to do, and it is the one thing I can say with certainty I have not half-assed. In high school, I used to stupidly say that someday I was going to have four boys because, you know, you can plan and choose that. I have loved kids for as long as I can remember, so I pursued jobs where I could work with them. I spent a great deal of my twenties teaching early elementary children. I saw up close and personal what being a parent entailed. I cared for and loved all my students as if they were my own, but at three o'clock, they went their way and I went to do whatever I wanted. I also got paid to plan activities, teach, and organize fun outings, known as field trips in the education world, while moms do all this bullshit for free. A few years in, I came to the strong realization that being a parent is not a joy ride. I saw that if you're going to do it right, you're in for some slavery. I saw the tears, I saw the sacrifices, and I saw how tumultuous life can be with kids. Somehow, between being a teacher and a footloose and fancy-free twenty-something-year-old, I blithely decided that such aggravation wasn't for me. I was adamant that what I wanted to be was a free spirit, tied down to nothing dependent on me for life. By the way, if you want to be a free spirit, don't have kids because they totally cramp that lifestyle. You can give it a whirl, though, but from what I know about free spirits, they do not stress.

Similarly, if you ever hear someone say that in order to be actualized as a human you need to have kids, that person hasn't lived a full enough life. They don't know what they are saying. No one is obligated to choose a life with children in it. Kids are not for everyone, and that is perfectly fine.

There are women who were born for this craziness, and they have my complete admiration! I call an elite group of them the Double Stroller Mom Squad. Any mom with a double stroller needs some kind of monument, perhaps one made of LEGO bricks outside a Target store. These ladies are changing two sets of diapers. Regardless of whether it was your calling or it fell into your lap, you embrace it, and by "embrace it", I mean you grin and bear it and wonder constantly if anyone can tell you're about to lose your shit. However, whether you are expecting your first brat or your fifth, once you become a mother, you're on the same platform as all other moms, and here, we all speak the same language. I look at my girls and I know that my life truly began upon meeting them, but I am also fully aware that it came to a screeching halt.

You're Just like Your Mother

Definitely, the way we parent has plenty to do with our upbringing. It won't be exclusive, as we are living in different times than when we were kids. If you are already someone's parent, you can pinpoint at least five things you are doing pretty much just like whoever raised you. If not, either you're lying to yourself or you moved to another part of the world and incorporated their customs. If your parents were lax with you, your parenting style is probably more relaxed. You are likely to count to twenty when asking your child to do something, and you have the patience of a sloth. Your kids are going to be annoying to everyone but you.

Regardless of your upbringing, once you are a parent, it is time to step up to the plate. In reality, life has privileged you, and you should never, ever take that for granted. Even while you are trying to poop and you have a toddler staring at you, remember...privilege. We get one magical holiday to get them back for all the shitty things they do and that's Halloween. That's our day to dress them up in something stupid and watch them collect all the candy we like. Then, once they are fast asleep, we devour it like sugar-deprived Cookie Monsters. It's a day that brings me so much joy!

My mother's go-to mechanisms were yelling and screaming—antiquated tools of the trade. I judged her, but I didn't get it. I wondered why she didn't talk more, not admitting talking seldom worked on me. Boy, do I get it now. She was tired of our shit! She was tired of laundry, of cooking, of working, of cleaning, of bickering with us about why we don't want to eat our beets or wear the shoes she picked out for us. It wasn't until I became a mother myself that I realized motherhood is just a lot of yelling with intervals of crying and drinking, wondering why the house is such a mess, and pretending you have your life together.

Remember the 1980s movie *Parenthood*? That's something real. Everyone should watch that movie before having kids. Despite our different walks of life, I can assure you, we all have kids who don't shut up. We are fully aware that there's a revolving door of endless laundry, and we can almost never find a Band-Aid when we most need one. I do agree that none of us will raise perfect kids, but strive to be a better parent than all of your peers so you don't feel guilty about judging their shitty parenting styles. Something I am sure you have heard and read a gargantuan amount of times is that judging is bad. But, keep in mind that everyone does it, be it secretly or openly. We are all constantly being judged, for the good and the crazy, too. I firmly believe that judging is how we set standards for ourselves. More on judging later.

Seven Things Every Child Needs to Hear:

I love you.
I'm proud of you.
I'm Sorry.
I forgive you.
This is your responsibility.
You have what it takes to succeed.

Sherrie Campbell, PhD

and one more from me…"because I said so, that's why."

Chapter 2
Raising a Tolerable Human

Whatever parenting techniques you encompass, be aware that you are raising children for society and not for your family's entertainment. Someday, they will not be fighting over who gets the top bunk or making slime with all of your household products. They will be out of your damn hair, planning their own lives, and ready to be productive members of society (let us hope). Raising a tolerable human begins in utero. Meaning, from the moment you become aware that you will be the parent of a tiny human, you must engage the part of the brain that confirms everything you will do as this person's dictator is for their own good. Subsequently, it is for the greater good of all who will coexist with him/her once you are "done." This, of course, will be after you have gotten over the bitter or enchanting shock of the positive pregnancy test(s).

Crushing Your Child's Dreams
You are going to be your child's first love, first teacher, first bully, and number one fan, even in situations where it isn't exactly appropriate. What does this mean? As it pertains to my life, and perhaps yours, too, I was raised with Tough Love. Whatever my parents' faults were, if I can call them faults, could be deemed causes of Psychological Peril, now in my adulthood. Maybe they worked too much. Maybe they could have been more sensitive to my feelings when I was growing up. I can look to find fault in how they chose to raise me, but the truth is, their way of teaching and disciplining me was the best way they knew how.

Today, as a grown-up, I can say with solidarity that I am stronger because of it, and I am someone who holds great value to the importance of raising respectful children. Bestowed on me are overly expressive eyes passed on to me from two generations, eyes that speak for themselves. As a small child, my mother need only glance my way when I was out of line. Her stare was enough to set me straight and tell me that was the only warning I was going to receive. It's a face I still fear. Now that's what I call parenting success! I am proud to say I will be able to pass this magnanimous gift on to my girls.

The realm of your duties as a parent is expansive, to say the least. You're going to be the first one on the sidelines of their lives, cheering them on, making them feel they can reach even the most unattainable dream. You better light that fire under their ass or be ready to blow it out full force if that dream is too far-fetched. And, no, everything isn't possible, so stop it with the clichés. I have a four-year-old, bless her little songbird soul, who says she is going to *America's Got Talent* for singing and says this with utmost passion. The problem lies in that she can't hit a note to save her life, and so, I have to crush that dream. Clearly, it's for her own good, but perhaps there is hope for her in the future and I'll have to eat my words. Crazier things have happened. My parents were pros at this technique and killed my astronaut dream early on, pointing out it would never happen for me because my math expertise was never going to elevate past the first grade. No permanent harm caused.

Child Amnesia

Nobody likes a spoiled brat, and everyone can identify one, unless he or she is yours because parents tend to wear Mom and Dad goggles. It's like beer goggles and dangerous as well, but in a different way. That's just the way it is, for the most part. If you want to be the kind of parent to buy your child's love, go for it. That's definitely one type of parenting style, but hardly anyone except a grandparent will tolerate your kids, not even you. In all seriousness, your presence and your time are of the essence. Give earnest attempts at finding time to enjoy simple pleasures. All kids are ungrateful. None of them appreciate how much money you spend or how hard you had to work for it. You can take them to Disney World ten times a year, and they'll barely remember, much less be thankful. Kids' memories do not become solid until about age seven, so consider everything you did prior to that a waste. Sigmund Freud coined the term "childhood amnesia" to describe the memory loss of the infant years. A 2014 article by Kate Gammon discussed new research regarding childhood amnesia:

> Kids can remember events before the age of 3 when they're small, but by the time they're a bit older, those early autobiographical memories are lost. New research has put the starting point for amnesia at age 7. (Kate Gammon, "Birth of Memory: Why Kids Forget What Happened Before Age 7," *Popular Science*, January 31, 2014)

Wait, so those hot ass summers spent sweating in Disney while toddlers screamed for no reason, as you try and get the perfect picture with Mickey for your scrapbook won't be remembered by them? I want my money back.

If you buy them the boatload of toys they throw tantrums for each and every time, all you will receive from them is a vicious cycle of more tantrums and complaints. They're also going to be too young to understand the joke, "Do you want some (string) cheese with that whine?" or pretty much any of your old, mundane mom and dad jokes. What your children are going to remember are the boring baseball games you never missed, the ballet recitals you attended, and the awards you saw them receive, even if they were just for participation. They will reflect upon family dinners, the songs you sat through as they danced and sang in the family room, the science experiments you helped with or did yourself while they watched, and the movie nights cuddled on the couch or in bed watching *Frozen* for the 55th time, to name a few. They will hold dear even the silliest of adventures. Those are the things we hold dearest in our memory banks, not the material crap that ends up tossed into donation baskets or garbage bags. Material things hold no substance in the grand scheme of childhood. Remember that when you are ready to take out a second mortgage on your house to fund Christmas.

Because I Said So

If you're worried that you are going to screw it up and be the cause of peril in your child's adolescence, you won't be alone in worrying. Cheers for having company in this almost inevitable journey of mental illness, for both parents and offspring alike. Just remember, if done effectively, everyone, collectively, can suffer in the traumatic experience that is family. In spite of how peaceful and understanding you are and how much of a "friend" you are to your child, at some point, they will resent you. They may claim to hate you, even, and when that happens, it will be momentous. You will then reflect back on the times you were so nice and wish hard that you had opened up more cans of whoop ass. So, don't be afraid to put on your Boss Pants, every day. You are the boss of the kids you birth. They are not the boss of you. When your thirteen-year-old, who still doesn't know how to wipe her ass, tells you that you are ruining her life, gently remind her that you are just getting warmed up. Dr. Nancy Darling underscores this for us:

> Laying out clear standards of behaviors is good parenting. Letting kids face the consequences of their actions and punishing them when they misbehave is a necessary part of teaching. Empty threats teach kids to misbehave. (Nancy Darling, PhD, "Why Threats Don't Work: Parenting Effectively," Psychology Today, January 19, 2011)

I have observed that parents seem to be afraid of their kids. Is it me, or are gone the days when parents would discipline their children openly and shamelessly? It seems normal for a child to throw a full-blown tantrum at a register because they aren't getting a toy they want. You must embrace phrases such as, "Because I said so, that's why!" You are the one who threw up for months on end while your ankles swelled into elephant cankles. You are the one who fought through hemorrhoids and leg cramps as soon as you were able to get comfortable in your pregnancy sleep. You sacrificed your perfect vagina and abdomen muscles to bring this brat into the world. Now, you say what goes. In the voice and words of the ever-funny Chris Tucker, "You are Michael Jackson, and I am Tito." You can be as "hippie" as you want, and allow your unique child to be themselves, but when you are out in public or at someone else's house, you risk that they will be reprimanded by people not as passive as you. It is my opinion—and by "opinion" I mean 99% fact—that children need structure, discipline, and some degree of fear; not of you, but of consequences. okay, of you, too.

If it isn't important to you to set boundaries and give yourself the place of the alpha, then by all means, allow miniature, unemployed people with toilet paper coming out of their pants run the show. Let those tiny humans dictate what they can eat and how much of it. Of course, allow them to throw tantrums everywhere they go just because they are kids, and by the time they're thirteen, you will be crying much like the parents on *Maury* saying things like, "I don't know how I lost control." There will be parents in the crowd, like myself, judging away. You lost control because you never really established it in the first place. I am a big believer of loving the child you have, not the child you thought you'd have. Every kid needs structure, at some level. Tell yourself that your baby was cut out for greatness, and teach them to believe every bit of it. Then, think about what you need to do as their guide to help them become the best versions of themselves.

Allow me to introduce a few people who were able to accomplish amazing things before the age of twenty-one. Think of them with admiration the next time your kid whines about having to wash the dishes, sweep, or pick up a mess they so enthusiastically made. Any kid who can overzealously navigate an electronic device is most certainly ready to embark in some good old-fashioned house chores. I'm pretty sure the names on this list were not spoiled rotten:

- Philo Farnsworth, at fourteen years old, drafted a sketch of what would later become the first electronic television.
- Joan of Arc turned a war around at seventeen.
- Blaise Pascal developed a calculator by nineteen years old.
- Mary Shelley published *Frankenstein* by age twenty.

My dad was serving in the Air Force Reserves and awaiting his first child by the age of eighteen. Ever since, he has been representing everything an exemplary father and husband should be. It's not too late for him to write his memoirs, but he has been quite busy serving the country and delivering mail for the U.S. Postal Service. Take a seat, Mark Zuckerberg.

Life experiences have yielded and paved the way for your new parenting job. Hell, you have tarried through this life collecting knowledge by facing your fears, failing, succeeding, taking losses, losing loved ones, and fighting for love, jobs, and sanity. Are you now going to allow a smaller version of you to make you feel inferior? Shame on you if you do. We must tighten up as parents! You have earned the right to lay down the law in your home as you prepare them for what is out there. You have omnipotence as the breeder of these individuals who wouldn't know right from left if not for you.

At the same time, while running your tight ship with equal amounts of fun and love, remember how important it is to send your mini-mes to school with basic values. School isn't the place to learn manners, for example. While some teachers are nice enough to try to raise some of their students, it is not their job. A television cannot raise a child. We aren't in the 1980s. An electronic device cannot raise a child. Those families whose kids sit at a dining table engaged in an iPad or smartphone won't know the damage they are doing until it's too late and you have a teenager who cannot hold a conversation with someone or even make eye contact when speaking to another person. I feel strongly about teaching kids to participate in small talk and to give their attention to the people who are present instead of hiding their faces playing games or, worse, hiding behind headphones listening to music.

I witnessed families in restaurants where each person is connected to a device and no one speaks a word the entire meal. I saw this for the first time when my oldest was an infant, and it made me sad to see humans having breakfast together and not even looking at one another. It shook my senses, and I vowed to not be that kind of parent, or person. We have choices. We are the people these young minds depend on for values.

I recognize there are exceptions and certain behavioral issues in children can leave caregivers exasperated, and it's easy to surrender to an iPad at the table. I recognize there are times when these devices come in handy. How else would I get through nail appointments, since my kids attend almost all of them with me? "We time" at its finest because "Me time" is almost nonexistent! Having excused my own reasons for smartphone usage, I can now alert the masses that there are far too many children nowadays crossing streets looking down at an iPhone, riding in shopping carts with eyes glued to a game, oblivious of anything occurring around them. More than obnoxious, I deem this dangerous. In my home, this is not allowed at a dinner table or with company. My kids know to not even ask me. It's a matter of fundamental respect, to be blunt, and a keen display of poor manners that plays a huge injustice in their socialization skills. As for these kids who are over the age of six and can operate all kinds of electronic devices with the same expertise as damn NASA employees, don't you forget what else they are fully capable of operating: cleaning tools. Put those kids to work around the house and position them, early, on the trajectory of being a team player. I recall an article I read when I was pregnant for the first time that said electronic devices should not be introduced before the age of two. Maybe I'm a square, but that kind of struck me as important information.

Equally, perhaps you have been the parent on the playground on the phone, not even bothering to look up, while your kid pushes another kid or tries to take their scooter without asking. It could be you have been the other parent having to decide how to go about dealing with someone else's intolerable child while the grown-up is entertained with a screen. Even if a child is taught some common core manners, kids may undoubtedly do kid shit and we can't be surprised at that. What is alarming is a mother or father updating a Facebook status, blind and deaf to what is happening right beside him or her. For example, I have had to pull a kid off my two-year-old daughter in a mall play area because his mom was on the phone, not even glancing up to make sure her son wasn't getting kidnapped! Her annoying four-year-old thought it was cute to climb over and push my baby more than three times. Unacceptable. Judged. I am not here to chastise anyone's parenting styles, but do not be this parent. This is just asking for strangers to go bat-shit crazy on your child. It's hard sometimes to know exactly how to handle the moments when your child steps over that imaginary line of insanity because, guess what? You may be right there with him. I don't live with any of you, and I don't have your kids. We don't possess the same amount of patience, and we didn't have the same upbringing. We live different lives and come from cultures far and wide, so fuck it. I don't know how you should parent your kid and neither does anyone else! If you whisk through a bookstore, you'll discover a rather eclectic span of books that promise to have a multitude of solutions for whatever parenting era you're in. You may gaze upon selections about labor and delivery, peaceful parenting, listening more, dealing with puberty, unruly toddlers, getting an infant to sleep fifteen hours, and what to do if you feel you just can't do this anymore, but you're always going to side with what feels natural to you, seldom actually heeding the advice set before you. Such is personhood.

It has always resonated with me that your children are a reflection of you. Growing up, my mother always made me remember this one way or another. It's almost like I have mental PowerPoint presentations of her speeches about the things I did wrong, and right, would be mirrored on her. She was so vain but so right! Having all these sentiments, I will be damned if I don't send out children into the world who are anything but polite, kind, and respectful to everyone they meet. Kids are not your best friends. They are broke tenants who depend on you for the tangible and intangible things they need to function as they begin to grow up and find themselves. They live in your home, contributing only hugs, kisses, and enough art to convert into 450 giant forests.

I totally encourage saying "yes" as much as possible, but do not be a stranger to the word "no," and learn to say it in many different tones and for almost anything. Most recently, I have been saying it in a British accent. You are going to excel more as a parent if you begin paying attention. There is a lot you can learn from other parents. I certainly have, and it is because I have drawn so much inspiration from other mothers that I have changed things I once did or incorporated something I didn't do before. Never be so fixated on what you read or how your family or friends did something that you are unable to see a different viewpoint and try a different way. Don't shut people out because their ways seem unusual or radical. We are all doing the best we can with the knowledge we have. Parenting, after all, is a string of hard misses, with some surprise wins that come in all sizes, but we have so much to learn, always. Maya Angelou once said, "I did then what I knew how to do. Now that I know better, I do better," and I can attribute this 100% to parenting.

On Children
Your children are not your children.
They are the sons and daughters of Life's longing for itself.
They come through you but not from you,
And though they are with you yet they belong not to you.

You may give them your love but not your thoughts,
For they have their own thoughts.
You may house their bodies but not their souls,
For their souls dwell in the house of tomorrow, which you
cannot visit, not even in your dreams.
You may strive to be like them, but seek not to make them
like you.
For life goes not backward nor tarries with yesterday.
You are the bows from which your children as living arrows
are sent forth.
The archer sees the mark upon the path of the infinite, and
He bends you with His might that His arrows may go swift
and far.
Let your bending in the archer's hand be for gladness;
For even as He loves the arrow that flies, so He loves also the
bow that is stable.

Kahlil Gibran, *The Prophet*

Chapter 3
The Messy Nest versus the Empty Nest

My brother and I used to make great messes all over our small living room floor. Whether it was playing teacher with my baby dolls scattered all over the sofas and dining room chairs, along with my brother posing as a student, or playing cars with the fifty plus Hot Wheels toy cars we owned, we were busy turning the house into one giant playroom. We used to build LEGO houses all day and cut paper into rectangles to make miniature store forefronts that our cars could park in front of. Block by block and car by car, our house became a city. They are some of my fondest childhood memories. I love that I don't remember my mother ever yelling at us to get all that shit out of the way. She let us play until we ended up fighting, which was inevitable.

Nostalgia for the Things We Bitch about
Messes are stressful. I understand how quickly one can lose patience at the sight of kid messes. I, too, have my days where tensions are higher than other days. There are those particular gut-wrenching days when everything annoys me, including my own shadow. You know the days where there seems to be an influx of toys and crap all over the place, and you blindly start yelling at everyone equally. On those days of shorter fuses, which may be associated with PMS, I want the messes cleaned up immediately. Surely, many moms can relate, or am I a psychopath in my own orbit? Regardless, I truly understand the importance of play and I allow it every day, even if I resemble Miss Hannigan, the orphanage caretaker in *Annie*. I loved that quirky character so much growing up, never expecting to resemble her in more than one way.

I do attest to losing my shit more than I probably should have at the worksite where slime was born or sand art was attempted, but I have decided to take it a little easier. Some days I don't succeed, and that's okay too. When it's more than one kid, it's obviously more chaos. I remember it being a lot neater when I was a mom of one. Is it just over at my place, or is the whole house a hamper? I don't get it. That makes for additional cleaning, and I don't know about elsewhere, but this makes the second decade my housekeeper doesn't show up, if you catch my drift/long sigh.

The other day, however, I was in a nostalgic mood. On this particular day, I came across a common sight in my house. It was a little plastic bowl, filled almost to the rim with water and a plastic doll in it. My kids like filling up cups and random bowls with water and having pool parties with small toys. Sometimes, they leave these water-filled objects in places where I trip over them or the dog passes by and all the water spills out. It's just one of the many annoying things they do, you know. It gets irritating, so I pleaded with my oldest to please not do this anymore. I asked her to please empty them out when they are done playing, for crying out loud! I ran into this bowl in the kitchen, and it almost spilled all over me as I reached over it to get my pre-workout powder. Instantly, I started to get mad, but then a wave of sadness came over me.

I looked around and saw lids of Play-Doh, glitter pens, and stickers stuck to the floor and realized that in the blink of an eye there won't be any of that for me to bitch about. Is it that I enjoy bitching or that I am going to truly miss it? I choose the latter. I envisioned a clean kitchen and dining area with not a single Barbie shoe or crayon misplaced, just boring adult stuff, exactly like an empty nest. In thirty seconds I time traveled fifteen years into the future and felt the emptiness of a home with no little ones who need me. I felt my heart shatter. I looked at that little doll floating in two inches of water and smiled a defeated smile. I picked my battle that day and decided I wasn't going to get upset.

I can recall going to a friend's house before I had kids of my own. Her one-year-old was in a playpen filled with toys, some big, some small, some were stuffed animals. The baby looked beyond uncomfortable in there, but she was trying to play with all her things. After my second glass of wine, I asked my friend why the baby was in there and if we could take her out so she could play on the floor. I was told it was because she didn't want a mess on the floor. Being that I wasn't a mother yet, I reasoned that maybe I didn't know anything. Instinctively, I felt like this baby should be allowed to play with her toys and make a mess for the time being. I guess you can say this was a first-hand encounter with judging other parents while not having any kids of my own. Eventually, it was time for the sweet child to go to sleep, and I didn't have to look at her in her cramped playpen, like an orca whale in an aquarium tank.

We're All in the Same Speedboat

After posting about the messy nest versus the empty nest on my blog, BilliejeantheDairyQueen, I was contacted by a mom eager to express to me how everything I said was relatable to her at the moment, and she proceeded to share with me her recent slew of emotions. She was adjusting to her two oldest kids being grown now and in their own worlds, the teen world, a scary place. She also had a two-year-old, but the capricious feelings she experienced from a semi-empty house were still present and difficult to manage. Everything she said convinced me I needed to write about this for all moms because regardless of where we are in the parenting world, at some point we will all face similar issues. It's exhausting, all of it, I mean. Every inch of parenting is demanding and even debilitating, but moms love to feel needed. We may have shameless increments of time where we fantasize about a life without children, but the thought of not having them around is heart-shattering.

Navigating through the parenting days, you start to wonder all kinds of crazy things. While you are zoned in on why there is a happy face drawn on the wall, the days will launch themselves into years. You will barely remember how your kid went from a crib to a toddler bed, much less how a kindergarten graduation turned into the first day of college. I am trying to live my motherhood days more on Easy Street. I tend to fall victim to a left eye twitch when all Barbie dolls aren't dressed to the nines and positioned perfectly in their Dreamhouse.

At the end of a long, tiring day, we're all in the same damn speedboat, and I say "speedboat" because that's what it seems like. Time is fleeting, yet we often spend a lot of it worrying about things we can't control and bickering about things that aren't really that important. I'm guilty of it as well. I'm trying harder to embrace all moments with more patience and grace. I'm striving to be conscientious of which moments are worth losing my cool over and which I should breathe through. I lack finesse, sometimes, in the mothering department, and I know I am not alone. I'm not telling you to rejoice at stepping on a LEGO brick, but you know…let us marinate in the reality that childhood days go quickly. Let's make a joint effort in putting the turmoil in soft focus from time to time to better appreciate the things that will be missed when we do reach the season of the dreaded empty nest.

Your children will be your greatest teachers, your biggest proponents, and the people who will directly and indirectly shape your life for the better. Between all of the amazing moments, those love bug kids will also be wearing you down, day by quarrelsome day. No matter to how many infinities you love them, your mind will wander to those kid-free days. You'll reminisce with fondness, until your daydream is interrupted by someone who can't reach something. If you never really noticed things like the moon or a ladybug's spots before, you will when you have a child. Children will teach you in their subtle and unpredictable ways to enjoy everything, to savor all moments, and to live in the now. Children do not have a concept of time nor do they understand words like "yesterday" or "the future." The present is where they live and where we should also spend our time. The most mind-blowing aspect of parenting is that just when you think you know it all or are coming close to understanding your purpose in life, you find a bundle of baby in your arms and BOOM! Mind blown. None of that other shit was your main purpose.

"In their innocence, very young children know themselves to be light and love. If we will allow them, they can teach us to see ourselves the same way."

—Michael Jackson

Chapter 4
Folding Fitted Sheets Doesn't Release Endorphins

It's not often we take mental trips to revisit our glorious childhood days because there are dishes piled up in the sink. For most of us, the best childhood memories we have are not having to sit in traffic, no seasonal allergies, and not paying bills. The memories of how much we enjoyed playing with dolls or cars seem so distant, and it's difficult to focus in on those simple pleasures that made us swoon with buoyant happiness. I feel that we must force ourselves to remember any part of childhood or of the "simpler days" that filled our hearts with joy. We should promise our adult selves time for self-gratification, time to feed the soul. If you have long forgotten, pay close attention to a child you may be close with—your own, a niece, a nephew, or one of your friend's brats—and notice how overjoyed they get when they are about to do something they love. Whether it's a bike ride, a trip to the park, a karate lesson, it's a beautiful thing to witness their little souls on fire, alive with excitement. Where is your excitement? Do you have a longing to experience something new? Do you keep a secret list of things you would like to accomplish? Many of us do, but that list tends to sit way under the grocery lists and the school supply lists. Those feelings of wanting more for yourself are important and should transcend into adulthood.

Kids Will Murder Your Spirit
Kids will crush your dreams if you allow them to. They will suck you into their soccer practices and piano lessons and your entire life will become like the movie *Honey, I Shrunk the Kids*, but you will be the ants and your kids the giants you are fleeing

from. You will find yourself staring idly at the TV watching the *Disney Channel* long after they have gone to sleep, for no apparent reason. Kids make you crazy. This is the reality, so my best advice is that you make yourself a priority. You matter. Your mental health matters. Releasing endorphins matters because you've got a long life to live, and you're going to be raising those needy kids until they are thirty, probably, since we are living in a time of smothering and babying our kids.

There may come a time when you are so involved in parenthood that you forget who and what you are. It happens to the best of us, especially stay-at-home moms, but you must rise above the excuses. I know by this sentence you have probably already decided you don't have enough time for anything else but degreasing the oven and separating the color clothes from the whites, but I promise that you do. Start slow, like with anything else. Walks around the neighborhood are free. Don't ever underestimate the power of a brisk walk with the sun and the clouds above you. Maybe you used to ride bike, or paint, or read a lot of books. Accepting that it is okay to deviate from the dirty dishes, rinse cycle, and mismatched socks will set you free, sort of, because if you're a parent, you're now serving a life sentence. Making time to engage in things that make your soul happy should be a universal endeavor. It has often been said that in order to take care of others, you must first take care of yourself. No part of that is untrue.

Come out from under the Pile of Laundry

I used to work several hours a day and juggle two or three jobs at one point. I understand all the directions in which one can be pulled and how draining it can be to work and then take care of kids. It leaves little time for fun or self-care because you are completely bombarded with responsibilities, all day, every day. That's no way to live! We trap ourselves. We allow others to entrap us, and then we blame the whole world when we are miserable. Such is personhood. Break that monotonous cycle for fuck's sake. Forge solidarity with yourself. Look out for signs that you need more, that you need a breather, and then strive to make even the smallest nook of time for you. I did. I know what it's like to inadvertently lose sight of who you are.

Stay-at-home mom life did this to me. My entire house—kids, pets, fiancé, washer, and dryer—chewed me up and spat back out an older, more worn out version of myself. The garden of grays isn't what perplexed me the most. It was what was happening to me on the inside.

You start to wonder, as you fold tiny underwear, where the other world you knew went. My second pregnancy really kicked my ass. Some days I didn't even want to get out of bed, which did not happen to me the first time. The first pregnancy made a mockery out of me, too, but I guess I was younger and still had tiger blood in my veins. I went back to work after three months and kept busy balancing my managerial responsibilities and my mommy duties at home. I worked full-time, looked after my house, and became a real adult, finally, at the age of thirty. I feel like I got the hang of it pretty well and truly excelled with all things maternal, except breast-feeding. That was a shit storm with the propellers on high (see Chapter 9). My second pregnancy was at thirty-four years old, nearing the age where you become maternal high risk, and I felt pain in my joints like never before. I was teaching voluntary prekindergarten (VPK) and teaching belly dancing twice a week, all the way up to two weeks before my due date. After that pregnancy, I became a stay-at-home mom. I had never worked quite as hard as I did taking care of two kids and a house.

My endorphins took to hiding when my back felt battered, and my joints were in constant pain. As many moms do, I was caring for my toddler, breastfeeding around the clock, carrying baby in the baby carrier, and embracing the newness and chaos of having more than one child and not being twenty. It was as if I had aged thirty years. It took me two years to realize I was allowing myself to feel beat up. I couldn't allow these kids to drag me down. I was taking all of this defeat as a personal affront. I'm the boss! I need to be running on all cylinders!

For me, it was Zumba that got my joints oiled again. It was dancing that brought me back to life. I have danced all my life, and it was what was lacking for me, but that may not be what is calling you. After I found my bearings and rekindled the flame with my wannabe Shakira hips, I slowly incorporated other things whenever I could—reading, meditating, writing—and, slowly, I found myself again. I was under a pile of laundry the whole time!

Baby Step Away from Mom Guilt

You aren't going to do it all of a sudden. It is going to take time, but once you make up your tired little mind that you want, need, and demand change, there is no stopping you. You have to acknowledge that you deserve this and that it will make you a much better parent. Notice I am not even referring to weight loss because as corny as it sounds, your happiness is not defined by your weight. Each of us has a responsibility to put our happiness on a pedestal as tall as we would for anyone else we love. We cannot allow life to swallow us into a pit of priorities. You're a very essential priority. Think of what happens in your home when you are sick! Complete and utter mayhem is what happens.

Making and checking off to-do lists is fine. Carpooling is cool. Clipping coupons and spring cleaning is great. Picking a password with at least eight characters, a capital letter, a symbol, three numbers…oh, never mind, that's just annoying. What I am trying to slap on your forehead is that you can collect all the adult gold stars you want, but you will still feel empty if you aren't nourishing your soul. Put all of that aside for, at the very least, twenty minutes a day.

Too often I talk with moms who tell me how exhausted they are (normal) and how they never do anything for themselves. On top of that, many feel guilty about being tired. They feel guilty about not wanting to play with their kids. The waves of mom guilt never relent. While it may be easier said than done, it is imperative that if you aren't going to let shit go, you allow it to subside every now and again. How are you supposed to be someone's little ray of light day in and day out if you are not happy in your own life? How are you supposed to teach kids the value of doing what they love and feeding their spirits if all you do is scrub toilets and rearrange condiments in the kitchen? That isn't life, at least, not the important part of life. Folding fitted sheets will not release endorphins because how do you even fold that crap?

Happiness Is an Inside Job

As much as I encourage the "do as I say and not as I do" way of life, there are other instances in which parents need to lead by example. If you want to curse in front of your kids but demand that they don't, cool. I'm not judging. If you want to eat Oreos every day but make your kids eat healthy most of the time, fine. You're the adult. You've earned that diabetes, but when it comes to your happiness, let them see you persevering and nurturing some of the things you love, besides being at their beck and call! At some point in the month, do something for you and maybe include them, if you absolutely must, but good grief, try not to! Do some yoga, knit, get yourself a canvas and paint some abstract shit, make a scrapbook, go jogging, do some gardening, take up a makeup class, refurbish a piece of furniture, and do things that make you feel alive, for goodness' sake!

There is more to motherhood than waiting for bedtime like you're about to cash in a lottery ticket. If you aspire for your legacy to be the sensational things you did as a parent, I applaud you because that's fantastic, especially if you did it without becoming an alcoholic, but damn it, challenge yourself to do more! We tend to bitch about how old we are, but one day we are going to wake up and realize that we weren't old at all. The years are fleeting and do not wait for anyone of us. Those stupid things we thought we didn't have time for we will regret not doing. The poignant thoughts will make it clear that we did have the time, we just had too many excuses and now we really are too tired, possibly, and on the stairway to heaven...or hell. Take those salsa lessons now. Go to the pottery classes ASAP. What I learned the hard way is that no one, not one person, will nurture your soul except you. Happiness is an inside job.

Mothers are the matriarchs of the family, not always front and center because we are the behind-the-scenes soldiers. If moms don't remember to buy soap and toilet paper, everyone will have to get hosed down outside each day. So much is expected from a mom, and even when it isn't, it's encoded in our DNA to give and give some more. I want mothers everywhere to know that it's okay to feel inadequate and even lonely. I think that means you are doing something right. What is not okay is allowing the almost constant demands of motherhood to consume you. You are not getting out of this shit that easy, so you must push forward. No one is going to yell at your kids quite like you.

Leave the Mom Hut Occasionally

I don't believe we all instinctively know the value of self-care. Often, however, we can identify when we most need it. We tend to defiantly brush it aside because the light bill is due, Mary has soccer practice, Ben hasn't finished his science project, and, damn it, the other one is still shitting her pants and she's almost three. I get it. It is not easy, but think of all the mothers who did what they had to before social media and smartphones! Can you fathom having to mom without the option of complaining on Facebook? We are spoiled. We can Google "best ways to cure colic" while our mothers had to figure it out or ask the neighbor and hope she had some sense.

It's a new day, so we can certainly figure out how to get one hour a month in to do something for ourselves. It's important to rediscover who you are outside of your mom hut. Stop feeling guilty about things you have done that will have zero impact on the adults your children will be. You're allowed to throw some of their art in the trash. How much paper can you possibly accumulate? It's enough the toilet is now a public place where you must discuss the consistency of today's slime as you poop and negotiate how much of breakfast will be eaten while you wipe.

Stop feeling guilty about eating candy bars behind their backs. You deserve every bit of those Kit Kat bars. Those ninja skills are going to help you tremendously during the teen years. Just kidding. Don't listen to me. I am nowhere near the teen years with my girls, and I am already pre-petrified of all that comes with that. I can't wait to see how I am going to handle it and how many parenting books I will be reading and burning. I'm also curious to find out if I will become an alcoholic or develop some weird tic. Oh, wait! I already have one of those. Every year around Halloween, I develop an eye twitch in my left eye, which tends to last through the holidays up until February. My kids' birthdays are in November and late

January, so the stresses of the holidays combined with juggling birthday ideas is excruciating. Every year I vow to "take it easy", and by September 1st, I am feeling the surge of the end of the year. Holidays were so much fun before kids. I will cherish those carefree me days forevermore. With kids, each holiday is an entire production that goes on for what seems like years! You are almost forced to celebrate whatever activities they do in school, then at home, carrying on to grandparents' houses, cousins' houses, and by New Year's you feel like ten trains and a bulldozer ran you over. Salutations to those people practicing religions that celebrate nothing. You guys are on to something.

In conclusion, if you are able to go out with some girlfriends, on a date with your partner, or by your damn awesome self from time to time, do not feel guilty. Enjoy that meal, that drink, that movie, whatever it is, without having to wipe anyone's mouth but your own. Relish those magical hours sans having to yell at someone to eat their vegetables or sit still. Have a good time listening to music you perhaps don't listen to with kids. Disconnect from the vacuum cleaner, and be grateful for the opportunity to flee the kingdom. Take a few minutes a day to just breathe, to put your feet on the grass, or to journal. You are entitled to a handful of minutes, even if it's in your closet stuffing a chocolate bar in your mouth as you do ten squats, or as you think about doing squats. The universe needs you to exude happiness. Do it for you. Your kids are cute, but they don't give a shit about anyone but themselves. This is also part of the masochistic research done by me.

"SHIT."

—Every woman looking down at a pregnancy test

Chapter 5
Half a Dozen Pregnancy Tests Determined You're Screwed

"It's a beautiful time. A woman's body is a fascinating vessel." (Insert the only cardio you'll want to do during your pregnancy: eye roll.)

Do you know what is most important to remember while you're wallowing in your pregnancy misery? We are not the only mammals who do it. Here is a list of fellow mammals that have it worse.

- Elephants, bless their hearts, are pregnant for two years, the longest gestation period of all mammals.
- Manatees are pregnant for thirteen months.
- Giraffes for 400–460 days!
- Walruses for fifteen to sixteen months.
- Whales and dolphins about sixteen months.
- Donkeys for fourteen months.

A shark is a fish, but, hey, their lives suck, too. They are pregnant for a whooping seventeen months! No wonder they're so feisty! Also, there is no one to bring them ice cream at 2:00 a.m. or pedicure their swollen feet.

It's Ten Months, Not Nine
I regard pregnancy, wholeheartedly, as a grand privilege because I recognize that many women are fighting battles with fertility. The gift of being able to carry life is one to celebrate, but, whatever, let's keep it real. Many women will agree that, sure, it is a beautiful time in the sense that you are embarking on a joyous new journey, unbeknownst to anything you have

ever known, but it is also a gross time. Most women only talk about how amazing it is to carry life but will delicately leave out that it can also be a nasty metamorphosis. It is a time of uncontrollable flatulence, swollen ankles and noses, engorged vaginas, extra dark nipples the size of dinner plates, to name a few unappealing changes. You'll be smuggling Oreos in your bra for more than ten months.

Stop listening to the mainstream crap that tells you it is nine months of pregnancy because it is all of TEN months. If you are one of the lucky ones who finds out they are pregnant when they're in their second trimester, you've had an amazing pregnancy thus far, and you are in for a shorter ride. Subsequently, you will spend less time dealing with pregnancy bullshit. Most women are in it for the long haul and find out when they are two weeks pregnant. From that moment on, you'll spend your days bored as hell, taking picture after picture of your belly from all angles humanly possible, planning a baby shower, and mentally preparing for this new life you know nothing about. You'll have to stay hydrated because if you don't, you'll get the worst, most random leg cramps.

As the weeks pass and your due date comes closer and closer, the pressure will increase in your crotch area because babies are assholes. They press on your bladder, use your rectum as a pillow and begin to push on your vagina with every fiber of their being. The most normal of human actions will become burdensome—sitting, walking, sleeping, talking, and possibly even having sex, although I strongly advise you stay horny because it is one of the few things you can still enjoy frequently and mindlessly. It also helps you go into labor during the home stretch.

For some women, the amount of flesh you carry in your bra will almost quadruple before the baby is even in your life, making it not only super uncomfortable but also painful on the vertebrates. You'll grab the attention of perverts everywhere, too, and since you are sober all the time, you'll take notice. You'll be told things like, 'Wow, you're glowing!" In reality, that's just grease. You are exuding large amounts of grease, but you look kind of cute in a hungry, anguished beluga whale way. Good luck if you manage to get pregnant just in time to be super pregnant during the equator temperatures of the summer.

That is over-the-top miserable, depending on where you live. If you have never experienced heartburn, there is a high possibility that you will now. You might become tremendously grossed out by the most bizarre things like toothpaste or peanut butter and oddly turned on by others. It's a whirlwind of confusion, except, of course, if you are one of those women who adores being pregnant. Who understands you ladies?

Pee on the Stick and All over Your Hand

Pregnancy is yet another burden women must plow through, like menstrual cycles, menopause, marriage, poorly done manicures, and bags under the eyes. I know very few women who jumped for joy at those two little pregnancy test lines taunting them, or now, the more intelligent tests that spell it out for you: PREGNANT or NOT PREGNANT. The majority of us collect 5–10 tests to be completely sure this is real life. What many women hovered over toilets in public restrooms, hotel rooms, and home bathrooms don't know is that no matter the shade of the pink lines, two of them mean that you are. Two of them mean you need to hang up your jersey like Jordan.

Two weeks after my 30th birthday, my breasts were sore and itching like crazy! I pretended this was the start of a peculiar flu. However, itchy and sore breasts did not seem commonplace to me since my periods didn't bring upon anything but light bleeding for four days. I used to be like the Unicorn of Menstruation, no pains and no PMS, floating by as my body disposed of my useless eggs. I try to be a bitch year-round to keep everyone wondering when exactly I have my period. Currently, I am the proud owner of an IUD ParaGuard, sans hormones, that makes me bleed for over a week. Apparently, the IUDs that release hormones give you more subtle periods. I say "proud" because it keeps me NOT PREGNANT. The fact that every month I have to prepare for a good hemorrhage turns me into Medusa. I do not have time for that, yet now I have to find the time.

Anyway, I had a few parties lined up, since it was my birthday month and none of those activities included reading the Bible in a meditation circle. I felt like I needed to take a pregnancy test, just in case. I demand outstanding merit for already displaying responsibility, which I did not want to have. I had my heart at my throat as I bought that stick, with my head pounding and my boobies itching! I could not wait to make it home. I had not told anyone that I suspected I was pregnant. Immediately, I felt I did not want anyone's opinion on the matter, and I was not prepared for celebratory exclamations. I stopped at a gas station in the early evening and asked to use the bathroom. Right there, I popped a squat, peed on the stick and all over my hand, and set the fucking stick down to wait. Every woman in this predicament knows this is the longest wait of all time. In the deepest parts of my soul, I knew I was, but I held on to a string of hope that the power of my mind and my incessant desire to keep living la vida loca, would give me one blue line. Still, I scarcely recall, a very exclusive, isolated part of me wanted the lines to be pink. Finally, the moment made itself present. There were two almost nonexistent lines, the lightest pink I have ever seen. I was confused and so, I went home and slept it off. In the morning, I bought two more. Then another and another. I took a couple of tests at work, some at home, and one at a friend's house. All of them had the stupid faint pink lines. They were not a defined pink yet because I was only two weeks pregnant. I cried and I mentally relinquished my March plans.

It's like when you step onto the Gravitron at the carnival, you know, the atrocious spaceship ride that spins you one way and then another while you are strapped standing up. You have to hold your vomit in because if you let it out, it will fly all over that damn spaceship and you'll probably get drop kicked by whomever it hits. That's what reading a positive pregnancy test is like. I was thirty. It was time to put on my big girl panties. I didn't give myself a choice. I had a good cry and then fixated my mind on the strong inclination that I was having a girl. Time to shop. I was happy and finally ready to grow up. Removing my belly ring was a huge rite of passage into adulthood.

People Want You to Get Fat

With your first pregnancy, you don't know what you're doing, and this transcends over to when you actually have the baby, making all firstborns poor, unfortunate guinea pigs to your ignorance. We do a wonderful job of covering up all the mistakes we make by later saying things like, "My firstborn is so special because I learned to be a mom. You taught me the meaning of true love." I guess that is true, but it is also a way of saying, "Sorry I ate potato chips right above you as you slept on me and the crumbs piled on your sweet head" and "Sorry I dropped my phone on your forehead while I checked Facebook."

Almost all first-time moms overeat while pregnant because you're told you are eating for two. People who want you to get as fat as they did will tell you this. Men will tell you this because the poor things don't know anything. Your mom will probably tell you this because she doesn't want you to die, but it is incorrect for a multitude of reasons. This automatically gives pregnant women the green light to shove as much food as humanly possible down the esophagus, with zero guilt and blame the baby, of course. Mind you, this fetus is the size of a plum and probably needs less than a grain of rice to live. From conception, babies take the blame for their mother's gluttonous behavior. It is like your body has been waiting a lifetime to hear those magic words: "Ready, Set, Fucking Eat Yourself Into a Coma!"

That "eating for two" crap is actually false and terrible to do. The women who turn into Ms. Pac-Man while gestating usually pay the price toward the end of their pregnancy and long after the baby is born. My aunt likes to tell people that she still has the baby fat from her third son who is now almost forty. It never fails to make me laugh. The second time around, you hopefully get your act together, either because your pre-pregnancy jeans are still nicely folded in a hidden place you don't speak of, or because of a scare of gestational diabetes, which is also a thing. You more or less learn that too much salt bloats, sugar will fatten, and overeating greasy foods will constipate and give you that amazing "pregnancy glow" also known as a grease mask. Still, you should indulge your cravings, which seem to be almost every minute, while simultaneously maintaining a healthy diet for the baby. See how this is annoying? After rolling my eyes for twenty combined gestating months, it's a miracle my eyeballs didn't get permanently stuck to the back of the sockets.

Pregnancy Is a Freak Show

Throughout the wary months of pregnancy, you'll watch your body do things you never thought possible, some of which will be disgusting things that you'll want to stop but can't, as discussed earlier. It's like a surprise everyday because you never know what you will get on any given day.

- Will I pee on myself today because I took a sip of water and didn't make it to the toilet?
- Will I get a muscle spasm that doesn't go away until I birth this creature?
- Am I going to get stretch marks, which are now called "stripes of courage"?"
- Is today the last day I can wear jeans?
- Will my hormones overreact and give me adult acne?
- Are my feet going to grow a bigger size?
- Will a leg cramp awaken me tonight when I am in my deepest sleep?
- Am I going to stab my spouse if he forgets to bring me pickles for my cereal?
- Can I stab him anyway?
- Are my rings going to get stuck when my fingers swell?
- Will I get a bunch of cavities because the baby will suck the calcium right out of my body?
- Is my vagina going to look like a Big Mac, hold the cheese, forever?
- Am I going to sweat profusely and stink like minced garlic?
- Will I cry at every comment, commercial, and thought I encounter today?
- Will I outgrow each and every bra I own?
- Will I have to start wearing Crocs, Toms, and other unde-sirable shoes?

The answer to all of these questions is, "Quite possibly, honey."

It's a freak show that is only training you for the real freak show that awaits. Ladies, I know this is hard to process if you don't have children yet or are in the very beginning of your preg-nancy. Don't be too frightened. Remember there are those strange specimens who love every bit of engorged vaginas and the circle of life. You may very well be one of them. The good news is that if you aren't, there is also a tribe for you of women who hate pregnancy as much as you. Come to the dark side...we have virgin piña coladas. It's not common to not have a "textbook pregnancy." You cannot compare yourself to your friends or what they experienced when they were expecting, even if you seem to have a comparable lifestyle. Some women float through the first trimester without as much as a pimple. Other unfortunate souls, like myself, throw up food they even think about way past the first trimester, like in the goddamn *Exorcist*.

Your pregnancies will possibly all suck, just in different ways. The best advice I can give about being pregnant is advice that had it been given to me, the likelihood of me applying it would have been slim. That is only because of the type of person I am. Here it is:

RELAX

(Oh, and keep a banana on your nightstand because it helps with the sporadic leg cramps.)

You versus Progesterone

When you are with child, it is you versus progesterone. Your hormones are only your friends in the hair growth department and not even because women have been known to grow beards during pregnancy. 'Tis true, friends. There's this nasty hormonal "pregnancy beard" called melasma that can show up in the form of patches on your face or one dark patch right around your chin area. It isn't hair, but it's a discoloration of the skin that is affected by sunlight and more prevalent in darker skin tones, so be cautious of how much sun you are getting on your face. It can be a very unattractive time for a woman.

As for your emotions, your hormones will undoubtedly affect them all. You'll experience at least five emotions at a time most days. You'll consistently worry that the baby moves too much or not enough, that you'll never lose the baby weight, that your spouse won't love you as much, and the list elongates as the weeks pass. Use this double-edged sword of hormonal rampage to your advantage, as the ball is in your court during this magical time. It's like a ten-month retrograde, if you will. These hormonal changes and even imbalances will affect your well-being and pretty much your entire experience. It is a time to be peaceful and focus on the health of your baby, who is picking up vibrations and listening to the drama of the outside world from the beginning. It is a chaotic time, which requires that you invoke tranquility into it. Basically, you'll be a living oxymoron, and that's enough to drive anyone crazy.

For me, baths with Epsom salt were a real treat. They would have been better with a lychee martini in hand, but that's frowned upon. Not only are Epsom salt baths relaxing, but the warm water will help if you have hemorrhoids or Braxton Hicks. Braxton Hicks are god-awful pseudo contractions that normally make their debut in the third trimester. Constipation is yet another pregnancy nuisance. Those can cause hemorrhoids and are much more insufferable than I can dare explain here. Water, fruits, and vegetables are supposed to be preventive for this, but I also understand how pizza, cupcakes, and fries may be what the "baby" wants. Remember that this baby doesn't care about you. She only cares about herself and where she can stick her little feet to cause you more strife. Deprive her of gummy worms and give that little shit some kale! Humph!

If you can find the time and patience, I feel meditation strengthens your mind and provides a great deal of tranquility during these somewhat tumultuous days. Tumultuous is just a sophisticated way of saying "annoying as hell." Truthfully, no one wants to hear your daily somatic complaints or how much pressure you feel in your vagina. I found that looking at positive photos and videos of successful births, such as the one you are aspiring to have, helped a great deal. In the Information Age, find the best information for you. Put some headphones on that belly and play Mozart for your baby, followed by Tupac because you want to prepare your child to be eloquent on the streets. Am I right? Fortify his math skills from the womb so he can do your taxes when he's five.

Eat healthy foods but also treat yourself. Be good to yourself during this time. Going to the chiropractor is a good idea. Taking a lot of naps is a good idea. Most of all, enjoy the last weeks you have left before you no longer get to think of yourself first.

Choose Your Own Adventure

There are various ways to birth a baby. I wholeheartedly believe that all birth stories are beautiful. However, births are even better when the mother made her own educated choices and did not succumb to those strictly provided by a family member or even a doctor. Figure out what kind of birth you want to have because people have a lot of opinions (some of which are good), and many doctors scare women to the core, making them fear what their bodies are designed to do. Never forget, you are WOMAN! The universe designed your body for bitching, jumping to conclusions, navigating toward damaged goods, and birthing! Form your own opinions from research you do, and be educated when it is time to deliver. Explore your options. It is paramount to be fully aware that there is more than one place to birth a baby and you're not limited to a hospital setting.

If you opt for a hospital birth, I advise you to be equipped with a birth plan in hand, which is a set of instructions, made by you about your baby's birth. For example, for me, it was stated clearly and highlighted that I wanted a natural birth and that a C-section was not an option unless it was a rare emergency. I stated several times that I did not want an epidural. I stated that I did not want a pacifier for my baby. The reason for this was that I intended to breastfeed. I learned that a pacifier can confuse the baby because a woman's nipples and a pacifier nipple are different, aside from other health concerns, like malformed soft plates and teeth issues. I did not want to fail, and I was already nervous about breastfeeding to begin with. I began to contemplate early on whether I was going to feed my baby this way because the opinions, testimonials, and advocates were everywhere!

The most important requests on my birth plan were fulfilled. If you do not go prepared, chances are others will take over your expectations unless you don't have any aside from going home with a baby and having the perfect girdle for afterward. I freestyled mine, typing on a regular white sheet, but I have since learned that you can find very useful templates on websites like babycenter.com and thebump.com. I looked them over, and they are equipped with everything you could possibly think of on the day of delivery. Admittedly, my daughter was, in fact, given a pacifier months later, as I tried to deviate her from the thumb-sucking she took to from the womb. These vices are tedious to deal with and we finished the thumb-sucking era at age six when she was mature enough to understand the dentist explaining to her all the consequences of continuing that disgusting habit.

Some women prefer to schedule a C-section, a doctor's dream, because in the United States, a C-section can go for $20,000! Since it is scheduled, the doctor comes in, cuts you open, and can still make it to happy hour. It is definitely less complex for the medical staff than going through all of the motions of a natural birth, but masochists like me who don't have any preexisting complications that may interfere with the natural birthing process prefer the savage option. I am terrified of enormous needles, especially in my back. The thought of that brings me to despair, and I learned in my ample research on childbirth that some women are left with lifelong back pain as a result of an epidural. I have to break my ass birthing and then have a souvenir of that brutality forever? No thanks. Additionally, hospitals make a substantial amount of money from your longer stay. You had surgery and cannot vacate the premises in two days. I cannot tell you how it feels or what the exact protocols are for a C-section because it is not something I have personally experienced. I have been told by other women that it is very painful since it is a surgery. You will need help for a couple of weeks after the surgery, as you will be stitched, weak, and adjusting to coming off medication. This makes breastfeeding a bit more challenging, but it is not impossible.

I must add, because I am a breastfeeding advocate, births such as scheduled C-sections and inductions can hinder the forthcoming of milk in most cases. The human body is quite a vessel, and it normally sends milk out the day the baby is supposed to be born. Although the milk is readily there, it isn't until the brain knows the baby is coming that it begins to allow the milk ducts to start their job.

Forty Is Just a Number

Often, doctors will tell a woman who is between thirty-nine and forty-one weeks pregnant that they should induce. Inducing labor unnaturally begins contractions so that the membranes dilate and the baby can be born on a date he was not intended to born, but it is a choice you have. It has become quite the norm to choose the baby's birth date. Still, you can choose to wait. Forty weeks is just a number unless your case is special and the baby's well-being is jeopardized. Babies aren't gallons of milk, so there isn't a defined expiration date. A woman can go over forty weeks. Think of our elephant friends when you are bitching at thirty-six weeks that you need that baby out. More likely than not, baby will come not too long after your due date. The very first lesson motherhood will teach you is patience.

In very rare cases, an emergency C-section is needed when it has gone too long after forty weeks. A C-section is also called for if the mother has uncontrolled diabetes, high blood pressure, or a condition where the placenta blocks the cervix, known as placenta previa. Please do not be unnecessarily convinced to be induced if that is not what you originally wanted and especially if it isn't necessary. You definitely shouldn't feel bad if you end up needing one, but Awareness of Your Options is the name of the game. I say this because many women truly do not know any of this, and when you do know, you might make a different choice. A few years ago, I heard the term "Too Posh to Push" being used in Hollywood regarding the recent rise in scheduled C-sections, not because of necessity but because it is common to just want to get the baby out and resume life as you know it. Waiting and pushing has just become a tremendous bother. I will repeat it one more time for the people in the back: I do not care how anyone births. I care that they had options.

Pregnancy is a time to reflect on all the rancid things you may have done in your life and accept the probability that you shall have to repay them all with the child inside of you. I hope this helps.

"I do not care what kind of birth you have; a homebirth, a scheduled cesarean, epidural hospital birth, or if you birth alone in the woods next to a baby deer. I care that you had options, that you were supported in your choices, and that you were respected."

—January Harshe from Coffee Sarcasm Solidarity Blog

Chapter 6
Labor and Delivery Means You're Two Steps Closer to Wine

Here we have a rhetorical question, as it pertains to my life: "How does it feel to give birth?" I have answered this question several times in the very same way, quoting a funny woman I once worked with: "Honey, it's just like shitting a pineapple." At the time it was said to me, I could not fathom such a thing. *Surely, it must be an exaggeration*, I thought, but negative! It's exactly like that, to be brutally honest. I can assert this now, times two. You shit out a pineapple with no Vaseline, and you are rewarded with a wet, wiggly baby who is ejected from what was your vagina but is now a vacant tennis court. Out comes a new life, as you basically give up yours. The end and the beginning, but mostly the end.

Should you choose to do it the way nature intended, this pineapple story will become very real for you. Otherwise, your thoracic area will be nice and numb. You can essentially watch a season of *This Is Us* without a care in the world, from what I am told about this birthing option. I can totally understand why women opt for the completely high on Mary Jane birthing route.

What Contractions Are Really Like

I'm not sure why no one reveals what contractions are really like. They have been compared to menstrual cramps numerous times. False. I think perhaps those make for some preparation, but your body ridding itself of unfertilized eggs is hardly equivalent. Contractions are more like incomprehensible stabs to the lower back, much like a kidney stone when it begins to inch its way into your soul, so do contractions. They start off innocent enough, just the right amount of pain to give you a heads up and make you feel brave. The body and the universe know perfectly how to trick us.

Funny enough, with my first pregnancy, a kidney stone is exactly what I thought I had. Having once experienced a dreadful kidney stone, the pain was similar. The old familiar dagger sensation penetrating my back was there once again, and since I was still one week away from my due date, I thought I was in for another stone. I began to research what happens in the event that a pregnant woman has to push out kidney stones but ended up going back to bed. About thirty minutes later, the pain was there again. I stood up and water splashed on the floor. I thought it was my water breaking. I panicked for three seconds, but it wasn't my water breaking. I just peed. It was dark in the room, and I had to actually bend down to touch it and smell it. Those last days of being pregnant are so goddamn awful. You become some sort of machine that can barely operate, and you're at the mercy of a fucking baby and her will to evacuate. When the pains were coming every twenty minutes, I finally came to the realization that I was in labor. The jabs began to feel lower and lower because the pineapple was on the way!

With my second pregnancy, I knew as soon as the first soft dagger hit my lower back. I was relaxing on the couch and FaceTiming with my cousin after getting a manicure and pedicure. We were chatting it up, and suddenly, there it was. That was at 4:30 p.m. Half an hour later, I was already sitting on the toilet with that horrible sensation of having to take the biggest shit, but it's really just a baby ready to cause some ruckus. No one tells you that either. Contractions begin to feel like the sensation of having to poop because the baby is now pressing on all your organs down there. It's literally one of the most annoying, intrusive feelings ever! For some, contractions begin after water breaking. I have never experienced my water breaking, but I did learn that if your water does break, sit tight because that does not mean you are in labor. Pour yourself a glass of water, juice, wine, or whatever, and get your shit together! The time is near. As a matter of fact, after your water breaks, it can still take a day or so. I also learned that you should do as much laboring at home and finally go to the hospital when your contractions are two minutes apart so that the hospital doesn't send you home. Taking a warm bath or shower as you labor and attempting to move around and squat prepares the body, the hips, and the baby for birth. It's a lot to remember. That is why I recommend meditating, becoming engulfed in the practice of how you want your day of labor to proceed, and being as mentally prepared as possible.

Train the Mind and the Breath Will Follow

I am not disregarding Lamaze classes. I never did them because I am stubborn enough to believe that nothing can prepare you for the fucking wrath being set forth at the time of labor. I recall thinking that I would probably become mighty irked at someone hovering over me telling me how to breathe. I guess I know myself well because during both births I would have breathed fire had I had a person telling me what the fuck to do with my lungs. NO! Get away from me! Let my own rage and misery push this kid out! Therefore, I do not know if those classes offer some exceptional benefits I missed out on. What I am confident in saying is that it is equally, or more important, to train the mind. I had faith that I would figure out how to breathe. Contractions are hardcore plunges that become more and more intense every hour. Then, every half hour. Eventually, there are almost no breaks in between and you begin to wonder if your entire ass is going to disconnect from your body. Yay, babies!

It's barbaric, really, but I promise you that it is doable, tolerable, and just about every single woman can succeed at a natural birth. I can't say all because there are exceptions and nightmares like placenta previa, issues with heart rate, and other complications that can infringe the natural birthing process. For the vast majority, the only thing that may interfere is your own fear. Women fear something that is natural. They are afraid of not being able to push a "big baby" out, when, in fact, it is an oddity that nature gives you a baby you cannot push out! When we hear of nine to ten pound babies, we cringe and then come the "Ooohh! Ahhh! Damn, that's so big! Oh, hell no!" But, if you stop and gaze at the mother, she is normally of an above average height and has very obvious childbearing hips. I know a 5'3" woman who had an eight-hour birth and delivered a ten-pound baby boy in her living room! Now that's amazing! Generally, the weight of the baby is an average of what the mother and father weighed at birth. Granted, there are exceptions for that. You may break the time continuum if you decide to eat pizza day and night. Also, your baby may surprise you by having the biggest fucking head you've ever seen. Who knows! At the end of the day, you never can anticipate what shit storm you'll be in the day you are in labor.

Don't Get Pushed out of Pushing

I wish all women trusted their bodies. I wish doctors weren't allowed to offer a scheduled C-section and early inductions but instead tried to teach and encourage women to birth their babies without intervention. God forbid they have to wait for a woman to dilate naturally because that could take hours upon hours and patience. There are dinners and events scheduled for medical personnel, so it is just easier to push women into a C-section, as to not inconvenience everyday life. Meanwhile, I feel these are pivotal moments in the life of mother and baby, demanding complete attention and respect, not a violent push into a rushed labor. Almost every mother I have spoken to who had a C-section revealed to me that she felt like she hadn't had much of a choice, for one reason or another. Regrettably, so many women are unaware of all the magical and phenomenal things that take place between mother and child when a baby is birthed unhindered and without medication because as early as thirty-five weeks they are warning you that if your baby isn't in position already, a C-section is a high possibility. Dr. Doris Peter explains the following:

> Research suggests that for childbirth, women pick their doctor first, not their hospital. Our goal is to get women thinking about the hospital, too, since the hospital you pick can play a big role in deterring your risk of a C-Section. (Doris Peter, Ph.D., director, Consumer Reports Health Ratings Center)

The C-section hospital ratings—all free—are available online at CR.org/hospitalratings. When the idea of a scheduled C-section was put on my lap by my OB-GYN at thirty-five weeks of my first pregnancy, I was prepared with the knowledge to fire back: "My baby doesn't need to be in position right now because I have about five weeks left. Even if at week forty she is ready to waltz out of my vagina, she could easily turn around back into Buddha position and not give a shit about my birth canal, so please stop trying to corner me into the C-section you're after. It's not going to happen. You are going to have to work that day, Doctor."

Every woman ought to have the confidence to speak up for herself and her baby and intelligently explain her concerns and uneasiness to her doctor. To an equal degree, doctors should have an avid interest in every woman's birthing experience, never dismissing her anxieties. When I told my OB-GYN that I needed to fax all of my paperwork up to that point of my second pregnancy to a midwife because I had decided to have a home birth, he voiced his opposing opinion. He told me I was crazy, as he giggled, and reminded me we aren't in the "olden times." Because I like him as a person and I know his sense of humor, I didn't go bat-shit crazy on him, but I knew well that he meant it all in a very serious way.

I Was a Belly Dancing T-Rex

Little did I know that the day of the birth of my first child, my doctor wasn't going to work at all because my daughter was eager to start her incessant urges to disturb my peace and came a week early. The doctor on call was known to give C-sections left and right, and I had horror stories about her embedded in my skull. When I ran through those hospital doors, my contractions were two minutes apart. I was a mechanical bull of predisposed readiness, and then, I was told to lie down. That isn't how gravity works. I knew that would ruin the twenty hours of labor I had been doing at home, standing and moving around my house like a maniac. I had been my own midwife, along with my cat who never left my side through all of it. We were quite the team.

Since the doctor was in another room performing a C-section, I was told to wait and lie down. It was terrifying. They plugged me into an IV, sat me on a bed, and I waited. I was told not to push. I stood and pushed when I needed to. I listened to my body, and I did what the fuck I needed to. I soon realized there was something terribly wrong and unnatural occurring. It was too much pain. It was bestial and different from what I had been feeling. I felt like my back was about to rip apart from my neck down to my ass. I literally almost fainted. I asked for water. I pleaded for ice and they denied it. I was confused and too tired to be angry, but the rage was there. I don't remember who I asked or how I found out that they had administered Pitocin in my IV because it's "protocol", but that is what was making me contract faster and closer together. It felt like one big wave of contraction, and I was livid, mostly at my damn self. In all the research I had done, I never read about the awful poison that is Pitocin and how it makes your uterus contract synthetically. This is to speed up childbirth so you can get the hell out of there and the next customer can come in. It is also an imitation of Oxytocin. Childbirth truly is a business, and I felt like just another number.

Once I came to terms with what was happening—there was a drug in my blood weakening me and no one would give me water or ice—I sincerely felt like they wanted me to fail. I could not allow it. I gathered up my strength, my balls, and my belly, stood up, grabbed my IV pole, and waddled into the bathroom. I felt like a damn Tyrannosaurus Rex about to tear up a city when I got myself up from the plywood bed they had me on. By this point, I had been offered an epidural about ten times. In the bathroom, I drank water from the sink and poured some on my face, which immediately gave me renewed powers. I squatted. I held on to the walls and breathed as I imagined myself dropkicking the C-section doctor and stabbing her in the neck with a needle full of Pitocin. Somehow, testosterone invaded my body by osmosis. I pushed and pushed. Eventually, I ruptured all of the membranes. It looked like they turned the lights on inside a haunted house. Bloody murder! I walked out covered in blood.

A nurse passing by the room looked at me and asked me to lie down, and at that point, I did. I was exhausted. She also told me not to push yet because, you know, you should totally stop your birthing body from doing what it is forcing you to do because the doctor is still unavailable. Of course, I pushed, and in a few minutes, another nurse walked by, saw a head between my thighs and called all the nurses on the floor to help me deliver my daughter. Another thing they don't tell you about birth is that you can never be 100% sure who will deliver your baby because unforeseen scenarios may present themselves. Michael Jackson played on my Nanopod, and there I was, having a baby. For a moment, all seemed fantastic and picturesque, as in what seemed like unison, I was pushing and following the nurse's commands. Almost as if from another dimension I heard the words, "Pass the scalpel," in a very monotone voice. I knew that concerned me and my vagina.

A record scratched in my brain, and I immediately stopped pushing to ask, "WHY?" Without an epidural, I would feel a slice, and I wasn't in the mood for that. The head nurse, directly in front of me, told me her shoulders were stuck. I kindly reminded her that I wasn't drugged and that I was fully focused and awake and could follow her instructions. Also, I belly danced for more than ten years, and I was pretty confident my hips could do whatever was asked of them. She gave me directions on how to lift my hips and sway this way and that way, and as I pushed, out came a pale, seven pounds, two ounces, nineteen-and-a-half-inch baby! I was in one piece with no tears, no stitches, and no C-section, and I instantly felt like a million bucks. It was glorious and it was badass.

You Will Remember All of It

While you may think there is no way you could do such a thing, it is chiefly because you have a preconceived fear of the pain and longevity of the birth. How long will it take and will you be able to handle the pain? What happens if you can't? To make matters worse, we live in a society that has made birthing something you just have to get done with quickly, so you can resume your regularly scheduled programming. Women are tricked into thinking they cannot do what their bodies are predisposed to do. This country only allows three months of maternity leave and our lives are incredibly fast-paced, making it seem like this also has to be rushed. If you train your mind to understand that women have been birthing from the beginning of time and that it is encoded in our DNA to birth babies, you'll feel the strength of a thousand women. There won't be a single person whose negativity can affect you. It will be otherworldly, and few things you accomplish after that will seem as gratifying.

If your partner is in the delivery room or living room with you, they will see things they can never unsee. The shock will be on a grand scale, and men have been known to faint, not only in movies, but in real life. If your spouse is a man, these emotions will come from a place of knowing they could never go through that themselves. That's also not up for any kind of debate.

Labor doesn't always go as planned. Even the most prepared mother can end up in a predicament she didn't expect or want. As long as the best is being done to bring baby earthside, that is what should matter and those are the precautions that ought to be considered. I have had the pleasure of speaking to many moms in almost ten years of parenting, and a great deal of them, in spite of them saying their experience was absolutely beautiful, confess that there are things they would have done differently had they known better. Even I hold these sentiments about the first time I gave birth. It is okay to mourn the birth you hoped for while still being grateful that you have a baby in your arms.

Don't think you're only going to remember the wonderful parts because you're going to remember almost all of it unless you were drugged. Then, a lot of your labor will be fuzzy. I cannot stress enough the importance of having a birth plan in hand the moment you sashay through the hospital doors. If you opt to deliver and labor at home, you are in cahoots with your doula or midwife, speaking the same language. I don't think it is arrogant to proclaim myself an expert in birthing. I have earned whatever right it is you get after having two kids two different ways, and if I can share this knowledge with women who actually want to know more, I will. I learned from listening to more experienced mothers, and I continue to seek refuge in the wisdom and personal stories of others.

My Home Birth

My home birth happened because I hated not feeling in control when I was in the hospital. Although I looked into a home birth for my first pregnancy, my iron was very low and I was experiencing full-blown anemia. It was so bad that I almost needed a blood transfusion. Needless to say, I was not a good candidate for a home birth. In 2013, after all the shit talking I did about never having another baby, I found myself looking at a new set of pink lines. This time, I did not take multiple tests. I also took a test from the Dollar Store because, guess what? They all detect the pregnancy hormone of HCG, so you don't need a Chanel pregnancy test to get an accurate result. You're welcome!

For my second pregnancy, I opted for a home birth where I could do things my way, cavewoman style, in the comfort of my own house. I would be able to have water, ice, nachos, and beer if I very well pleased. I found an amazing midwife with whom I instantly clicked. After ensuring I was a good candidate for a home birth, my fiancé and I knew this was a great idea, not that his opinion exactly mattered. We rented the pool, drove to her house weekly for checkups to monitor the baby's heartbeat, check my iron, and prepare for the day. I began reading birth stories and watching videos and learning the science behind birthing at home versus in the hospital.

Meanwhile, I was still seeing my OB-GYN, still deciding what exactly I wanted to do. It was a slightly less miserable pregnancy, less stressful, less vomiting, and my anemia was not debilitating my iron as much as before. I decided that I was going to switch over to a midwife when I was about twenty-nine weeks pregnant. When you know you have options, things don't seem so intimidating. The day we walked out of the midwife's house carrying a birth pool was the day I knew it was for real. It was something liberating, forcing me to break the calamity of any doubts and birthing fears I may have been suppressing. I was unleashing myself from the untrue idea that hospitals are the safest places to birth, and I was finally following with my gut. I dismissed all superfluous anguishes right then and there.

When you say you're going to have a baby at home, most people get all weird and ask if you are sure about what you are doing. They begin to put their own fear on you, almost like a blanket of bad vibes, but they don't mean to. It's just fear of not knowing and immediately anticipating the worst. My own mother tried to convince me not to do it that way, and she and her siblings were born at home. She was not invited to participate in my home birth. She made it clear that she was capable of calling the ambulance and I believed it! I also would not have been able to deal with her pacing back and forth in my living room, rosary in hand. Just the thought gives me anxiety. Now she sings my praises and tells everyone that a water birth is, by far, the best way to birth. Gotta love our mamas. Someday, we are going to be just as meddling, opinionated, and relentless as them. If you don't think so, pay attention to your everyday mannerisms and quirks as a parent. We're halfway there!

Whenever I am confronted with inquiries about a home birth by women who are either curious or have actually contemplated having one themselves, the main thing I try to make them understand is that it isn't something unusual. It is also normal to fear what you do not know. The fear that something can go wrong or that you may not be able to go through with it are two of the biggest concerns. It's understandable, but remember that women have been birthing that way for centuries, with far less knowledge and tools.

In the last weeks of pregnancy, baby's heartbeat is regularly checked and those numbers documented. Once in labor, the midwife continues to check the baby's heartbeat to make sure it is consistent with what she has been monitoring. Any abrupt changes and the birth can swiftly turn into a hospital birth, so you see, there is science to it. There are many precautions. At the end of the day, a doula or midwife isn't going to take their chances if they are unsure about the turn out. My midwife is also a registered nurse. She was prepared with the knowledge and capability to sew me up if I tore, administer CPR to me or baby, use her hands to help deliver the baby, and control a hemorrhage, for example. It is quite rare that there will be a complication on a grand scale if you have had a healthy pregnancy and you aren't experiencing any health issues.

The Ultimate Pool Party

My home birth was ten hours. The first couple of hours I labored through contractions around my living room area and in the guest bathroom. They were still mild and tolerable. After that, I decided to change the scenery and go to my room, which was upstairs. I don't know what made me want to walk up the stairs, but once there, the contractions began to get closer and closer. At that point, I was stuck on the second floor of the house with pains so hard I could hardly see straight. I called the midwife, Eunice. She asked me why I wasn't inside the birth pool yet, so it was then time to waddle down, with the attentive and wide-eyed daddy-to-be behind me, and begin the greatest pool party of my life.

I admit that by the sixth hour, I was very tired. The continuous waves of pain were intense. The incense and candles got on my fucking nerves, and the only thing keeping me semi-sane were the Grammys on TV. That was short-lived because after Pharrell and Stevie Wonder's duet, I was back to my current crazed situation. My freshly manicured hands and feet were shriveled like raisins, and I was about to grow gills. I was over it!

I looked at Eunice and I said to her, "I don't think I can do this." I meant it, too. It was crazy.

She replied with a very soft, "You have to. Remember why you wanted to do this in the first place."

That was all the encouragement I needed. I started to have little pep talks in my mind until I regrouped. I found myself filled with renewed strength and power. As a powerful woman once eloquently said, "Where there's no struggle, there is no strength." That woman is Oprah, by the way. Oprah does not have kids, though, because her intelligence is superior to mine, but I feel like she would give this advice if she were a midwife.

When choosing this type of childbirth, your mind has to be all in. All of the motivational life quotes you have read must become one. You have to transform yourself into the Dalai Lama of birthing, believing completely in yourself and your body. You must disregard the naysayers and pretty much keep a lot of your amazing birth plans between yourself and your spouse! This is not superhero shit, but it kind of is. My cat delivered seven kittens in my patio, unassisted, with no epidural, and with no ice chips. I'm telling you this because I totally believe in the strength and power of women, and felines too.

Ruthless and Beautiful

Although utterly different, both of my births were amazing. They were exhilarating in distinct ways. Both nearly killed me. Neither one was easy, but each one was beautiful in its own ruthless way. I didn't shit myself during either one, so that's a plus. Many women fear this more than actual labor. You can choose to get an enema a couple of days before your due date if you are worried about it happening. However, I can tell you with confidence that when the moment comes, you will not care who or what you shit on or where, even. It is literally the last thing you are stressing. Labor and delivery is an awakening.

Once you know you are in labor, the party is over. The napping is done. The walking the neighborhood a gazillion times to try and go into labor is over, and it is time to rise to the occasion. You're going to embark on a steadfast journey into a different dimension, and throughout it, you are going to learn who your true friends are. I won't expand too much on that because I trust the wheels in your head already spun. Your spouse will probably be running around like a headless chicken being totally useless, and you'll be nervous and possibly peeved by their ineptitude to birth the child for you. Still, it's show time and, hopefully, sooner than later, you will have a new title. Upon arriving to the hospital, you'll have to be prepared with a birth plan, if you have one, car seat installed to take the nugget home, a bag with all your crap, and a camera to begin the joy of blinding your child with photographs hourly. Some mothers will argue that labor and delivery are, by far, harder than actually being pregnant. I cannot agree. There have to be at least a handful of moms who say the opposite.

There is nothing as sublime and noble as a woman sacrificing her mind, body, and soul to bring another human into the world. It's only the beginning of a surplus of crap you will have to sacrifice as a parent. To birth a human you know nothing about, of whom you haven't any predisposed notions, is stupid brave. I mean, the only thing you truly know without a shadow of a doubt is that you will be coordinating outfits with him or her about three times a month, more if there is a holiday. Those cute photos will cost you, though. You will first have to endure ten months of torture as you transform into a hangrier, more irritable version of yourself who hates everyone. Then, as if that wasn't enough, you'll also have to endure the turmoil of getting that alien out of your belly and into your tax deduction. During all that you will have to answer at least twenty questions a day about how you're feeling, what your plans are for names, what is the gender, where the baby will be born, and so on. Every damn day. Not an easy feat. What's even worse, you'll have to hear the resounding words of, "It'll be worth it in the end," from almost everyone, to which you'll respond inside your head or out loud, every single time, "Yes, but right fucking now, this sucks woolly mammoth balls."

Still, one of the hallmarks of parenting is that in about five years, you'll have a kid who can take a decent picture of you if need be. It's the little things.

"What I know about all Moms for sure is that we are all one 'MOOOOOOM!' away from a white padded wall."

Chapter 7
Motherhood Is a Sport

In the gauntlet of motherhood, we are athletes. This shit is a sport! You will spend eighteen plus years crawling through the scariest hood that exists. We don't get tools or protective gear or a manual. We are not offered any real training in this department, yet we are expected to excel at something we know nothing about. Our initial training is through the battlefield of our own childhood experiences. One moment we are chugging mudslides on the beach, celebrating absolutely nothing and the next we're starting college funds for infants and choosing mobiles and baby monitors. The initial entrapment into the parenting abyss is almost like solitary confinement. Outside of our innate motherly intuitions, we have sheer luck.

Celebrate Mom Wins
Oftentimes, that infamous "mother's intuition" isn't working up to par. We get super tired and drained because of the one hundred roles we are expected to play daily. This is when we have to remember the supreme mothers of the past and marvel at their excellence. Who are those badass women who mothered with no social media outlets, no Target, many with no car and no time for luxuries like Netflix, even if it had existed.

As my condescending aunt says in jest, but she's actually not joking, "In my day, we didn't have time for postpartum. We had chores to do, a house to maintain, and other kids to take care of. We had to iron clothes for our husband, sew, cook three meals a day, and take care of the other kids. If I had been moping around sad, who would have done all of that?"

Interesting question. My aunt comes from a time when an elongated cord connected to a wall as you spoke into a large phone from a landline. Years of research and intense scrutiny on postpartum have defined it a serious ailment for women all across the globe. I may laugh at her prehistoric humor, but I know damn well women battled postpartum, mostly silently, then, as they do today and it's nothing to make light of.

The sport of Motherhood elicits a unique type of commitment that even on your worst, most anguished day, you must still perform. There is no bench either. That's reserved for dads. It's grueling in the sense that your teammates are selfish assholes, and you must push through because you can't necessarily push them over a cliff. Notice I said "necessarily." Some days it's like you aren't even on the same team. No matter how many pep talks you give, someone will oppose and play their own way. Your mental and physical strength will be constantly tested during whatever phase of motherhood you are plowing through. Whether you are delivering a squishy eight-pound baby, carrying a sleeping, twenty-pound toddler on your tired body, listening to a grade school child ask you where babies come from and if Santa is real, or cringing at a middle schooler who is beginning to ask some of life's most daunting questions, there will always be something new. It could even be a teen in high school learning to become more independent and everything in between and beyond, since the "fun" is infinite! It's a relentless and savage sport.

Some days, you'll experience victories, also known as Mom Wins. It can be a big thing, like a child graduating or winning a spelling bee, or something small, such as a toddler eating all their vegetables. Take all the wins you can because other days, you'll want to throw in the towel. You know, one of those wet towels you forgot about in the washing machine that smells like pond. Undisputedly, mothers are true committed athletes with acute sportsmanship. You keep rising, cheering your team on, fervently, day after day and year after year. You document everything, be it with photos, journals, or mental pictures. You know every detail about each kid and each event, yet there are days you won't know where the keys are or whose birthday party you're about to miss this week. It's a balancing act that never allows for a rest, for even if you are on a light "life break", the mom worries are still in the back of your mind trying to surface and ruin your peace. I feel like this is one of the hardest parts to adjust to as a new mom, and even as a weathered mom—the sense of always having five hundred web browser tabs open in your mind, and most are for people other than yourself. You don't exactly get to sleep again, either. I mean, your eyes close but your brain is always awake thinking and worrying about the little lives that have taken over in every aspect. We sleep like dolphins, with half of the brain asleep and the other half awake, looking out for predators. The predators, obviously, are the children.

Reassure the Rookies

Motherhood is a sport you don't get paid to partake in, although you're the champ of all champs, solving problems, delegating weekend plans, showing face at parent conferences, and volunteering your free time to shit you would rather not do, like birthday parties and play dates. You are recompensed for all your labor on assigned days, such as Mother's Day. On this day you are treated to handmade cards and other useless art you'll cry over because its cuteness pulls on each one of your heartstrings. Maybe if you're lucky, on Mother's Day, you'll get to drink your coffee warm, instead of cold, since it was not meant to be cold. However, chances are high that you'll have maternal responsibilities, nonetheless, and you won't, in fact, get to shit, shower, or shave uninterrupted. It's a commemorative day, kind of, so there's that.

On regular days, you will receive hugs and wet kisses in exchange for everything you are supposed to do as head coach. This is sweet, but it doesn't pay the daycare and Christmas bills. It can become dangerous, even, because you may reach a point where you are wholly dedicated to everyone else and you neglect yourself. It can feel like you're in a lonesome place, since it is possible you keep your troubles to yourself. I urge you to consider keeping a perpetual sense of humor, for you will surely need it every waking moment. Whether you are picking your battles or in full-on combat, laughter will keep you sane. Wine will too.

Throughout motherhood, you will be forced to surrender one or more of the following parts of your entity, at least for a bit: sense of self, spirit, body, career, sanity, boobs, hobbies, and simple pleasures. It all starts with pregnancy when you must give up cocktails and skinny jeans. We're pretty amazing in our early on dedication to a fetus because we know that women back in the 1950s didn't give up martinis. Some mothers lose one or more of these never to be found again, but these are things we gamble when we decide we are ready to grow up and have babies.

As you gradually become better at this sport and gain some mama confidence, don't forget about the rookies. Those new moms you see out there with constipated smiles need your reassurance and perhaps even your unsolicited advice. It is your duty to press upon them your unruly and biased opinions. Hopefully, you are providing good advice, but even if you're not, they'll have to find their own fucking way, just like everyone else. This sport is merciless, but we get by one small victory at a time, one pity party at a time, or one adult tantrum at a time, which normally involves an adult beverage, or six. It could also involve retail therapy or actual therapy. Do what you must, and don't concern yourself too much with judgment from outside parties. The good news is you can always get a dog, if you don't have one. I once read that parents should get themselves a dog before their kids are teenagers so there will always be someone home who is happy to see you. Makes sense.

Motherhood Magic

Just like in any other sport, you are allowed to cry, feel defeated, and crave attention. You may also wear the same uniform every day, if you like. My daughter calls my sweatpants "soggy pants", and I crack up each and every time. When I am not in a tank top, braless, and wearing one of my many soggy pants, they "ohhh" and "ahhhh" and tell me how pretty I look, and that feels better than a compliment from my fiancé, to be honest. Don't forget that you are human, too, and you also need to do things that ignite your soul. Changing diapers and figuring out teething has begun are not things that ignite the soul. Hold on to the notion that your children will forgive your shortcomings. Regardless of how excruciating it is some days to hang out with them and regardless of how downright draining they can be, they really do want to see you happy. They sing your praises behind your back, and they are watching you ever so closely.

Too closely.

There is basically nothing they think you cannot do. No pressure, right? But, you know what? They are usually right because mothers figure it out, somehow. It's like some superhero force envelopes you, and come hell or high water, moms swim, leap, backflip, and deliver. Once you become "MOM" there is no such thing as "needless worrying" because all types of worrying can be justified. Don't even worry about your excessive worrying because that may invite along a panic attack. Just continue to worry because that's what you do when you are raising kids—worry relentlessly forever! This sport doesn't allow for early retirement because you were injured. You can be ten margaritas in and suddenly prop yourself up into a thought about how last June someone said something really mean to your kid and now you have to find that kid 365 days later and steal his puppy.

Speaking of how motherhood is a sport, I actually like to compare it to a plank. Have you ever held the plank position during a workout? It's horrid and that's kind of what mothering kids can be like. It's holding a plank for eternity. Parenting through the teen years, I imagine, is like holding a plank for eternity while also trying to hold in a fart.

You'll find that there is some sort of mystical reservoir of patience, love, strength, and fortitude that somehow, some way, shows itself when you need it most. For some of you lucky ones, that may be attributed to coffee mugs rimmed with Xanax, but for the most part, it's just Motherhood Magic. It may not be what you necessarily signed up for, but you're here for it now and so are your kids. There is an astounding beauty in the chaos. You are basically dedicating your very existence to raising little reflections of you. How masochist of you. Don't ever doubt your skill in this game, not for one second. Your teammates can sense weakness.

Oh, and dads, when you aren't on the bench, you do great as referees.

"You go through big chunks of time where you're just thinking—'oh this is impossible! oh this is impossible!' And then you just keep going, and you sort of do the impossible."

—Tina Fey

Chapter 8
Discipline Is Not a Democracy

Your child was born to love you, so they love and worship the ground you walk on. Use this to your advantage for the few years you have this abundance of love, devotion, and unbiased admiration. You can use your weapon of choice to mold your disciples into what you want them to be. Your strategies are readily shaping what kind of addictions, epidemics, and deplorable behavior your kids will fall victims to: obesity, drugs, being a litter bug or a sociopath....

There is no end to the possibilities of what your kid can become under your rule! It is vital to be controlling, something that cannot be helped anyway, right? It's okay to not let them lock their bedroom doors. It's all right to demand certain things from them and to hold expectations of them, but unless you are diligently antagonizing, don't expect it to get done.

Let's face it, you had a choice. You chose to grow up and become someone's parent, while probably still needing some kind of maternal affirmations of your own. Perhaps you came close to backing out, but you didn't, and no one has to know if you secretly plotted ways to get out of it. So, now it's your turn to take out your frustrations, complexes, failures, and repressed childhood issues out on your offspring. After all, that's what our parents did and we turned out mediocre. We're in a revolving door of repeating mistakes and making sure our kids pass theirs on to their own children.

Because I care about you, I am going to be nice enough to impose on you some plausible parenting tools.

Manipulation

You are probably more skilled at manipulation than you even realize. It has quite possibly been an emancipator in your relationships, both personal and career oriented. No need to feel ashamed. All is fair in love and war, and parenting! It's now time you incorporate manipulation into your parenting style before your kids use it on you. I find that children at the ripe age of two are already exercising their feeble manipulation skills on their parents, but parents are too busy being blinded by their cuteness to see what is happening.

You must be creative and adept at discovering what kind of kid you have. Some of these brats have superior intelligence, no matter how dumb they pretend to be. Remember, you have decades of experience over them. They could never outsmart you! If you allow them to rule your life more than they are already meant to, you're probably going to end up needing one of those British nannies you see on TV. They come into people's houses with one task and one task only: destroy unruly behavior! They abolish it 100% by yelling and insulting everyone, pets included, all while utilizing a fabulous accent. I can't help but wonder about families like that. How do you get to the point of losing total control of people you birthed? How did you allow these little shits to become superior? Remember what I said about judging? There's an example of when you may freely judge with no remorse.

Bribes

This has been a reliable source of manipulation from the very beginning of time. Even the ancient Greek Olympians bribed their way through matches. There's absolutely no reason why it cannot succeed in the parenting world. I have witnessed many parents use it extraordinarily, myself included. Bribing has a 100% chance of meeting your demands in a timely manner. Remember that bribing isn't limited to promises of toys, candy, and other sweets. It can escalate to negotiations for far bigger rewards, such as trips you're not going to go on or money you don't have to give them. Bribe them anyway. They are stupid, naive kids who must learn never to accept a bribe. How else will they learn if not by your tough love parenting and lack of empathy for their feelings? They can begin to have feelings when they are adults or when they pay their first bill. Every tear they shed is for their own good. Bribing is one tool that doesn't have an expiration date. You can carry this through every phase of growing up, way past the teen years if you put your mind to it.

Comparisons

This is a real douche bag move, but I'll lay it out anyway, for emergencies, you know. Go ahead and flamboyantly compare your children to one another. Point out how one is so much better at everything than the others and will likely be the one to excel beyond the others' accomplishments, both in their career and in personal relationships. This will provoke the others to work harder at earning your love. All parents who raised kids from the 1970s to the 1990s would back this up, except they can't because now they are grandparents. Grandparents are not the badasses they once were. Now, they are the enablers, the softies who can't stand to see their precious grandbabies being reprimanded or scolded. They are not on your team either. They work for your kids now.

Life Threats

I won't say much about this to avoid misinterpretation. Some of you don't know how to party and have probably already cringed more times than you'll admit throughout the course of this book. I will say this, though, my mom gave me life and she threatened to take it away a few times. I admire that about her. The reality that I believed she had it in her to send forth the Grim Reaper on my ass kept me on my toes. The key is to make them believe you are capable of taking away their young lives without ever actually doing it, or even saying the words. I hope you follow suit.

Evasiveness

Never give your child a straight answer. They don't deserve it. Just think of all the answers you are still waiting for life to deliver to you! Use "maybe" as often as possible, but always make it sound like it is leaning toward "no". Be consistent with what you say you will or won't do. The worst thing you can do when disciplining a child is to tell her you are taking something away or not taking her some place, for instance, and then go back on your word because you're weak. Parenting isn't for the weak. Say "yes" as much as possible, but throw in some solid "noes" and make them understand that "maybe" also means no, but in a nicer way. Make them wait for answers, too, until they're almost in tears or until they are actually wailing. This is a small, satisfying asshole parent move that feels kind of good. Hey, we have to deal with their undying toddler-kid-preteen-teen-adolescent asshole moves!

> Intolerable Human: Can we go see that new movie that came out?
> Parent: (long, silent pause because your ignoring skills are even better than theirs)
> Intolerable Human: MOOOOOOOMMMMMMMM, can weeeeeeee?
> Parent: I don't know. I have so much stuff to do. Maybe. (Insert evil laugh in your head.)

Mean Mommy Advice: Have you ever tripped your kid as they were walking by? Try it. It's a fun and quick way to treat mom angst.

Chapter 9
Breast Is ~~Best~~ FREE

What credentials make someone an expert in something? How much research, experience, or years at a formal school need I have in order to call myself a Professional Lactation Dairy Queen? I know you cannot be a Lactation Specialist unless it is tied to some sort of medical degree and/or some extensive classes and hours of free labor. Yet, I am going to be ballsy and label myself a Certified Dairy Queen after nine years, two breastfed kids, and four years total breastfeeding kids! Trial, error, tears, blood, and research of my own has led my breastfeeding activism to help many mothers pursue a breastfeeding journey. Did I mention blood? These boobs have been through hell and back, and while I earnestly was never exactly rapt to start oozing milk out of my boobs, I felt like I was going to do what I had to do. Plus, can you imagine the amount of judging my own mother would have evoked upon me? She who breastfed both my brother and me. Normally, I would advise to not take to heart other people's parenting advice and do what you feel is right, but this topic is of utmost importance to me and to all babies, past, present, and future.

I have enthusiastically advised a diverse realm of determined moms and played the part of lactation consultant more times than I can recall. Regardless of whether a woman is expecting her first child and is being asked by every single person if she is going to breastfeed, a second- or third-time mom who perhaps failed before and wants to try again, or a mom who knows the ins and outs of breastfeeding and just wants a few tips, few things in this world bring me as much joy as being able to guide and successfully encourage a mama to feed her baby her liquid gold. I have made myself accessible through the years for free. It is a no-brainer that I include a chapter dedicated to this wonderful, nourishing organ known to us as breasts. I am positive that my activism toward breastfeeding has brought upon a multitude of eye rolls, but that has never stopped me from sharing intimate photos of myself with baby latched on, facts I found on reliable websites, and more picture of my baby attached to me like a little chimpanzee.

That's What These Boobs Are For, Lady!

Whether your breasts are natural or enhanced, they were placed on your chest for one reason and one reason alone—to nourish babies. Sadly, society has skewed this reality into making it seem vulgar. How dare a mother feed her infant her breast in public? GASP! Yet, if in the same location, a woman walks by in a halter top or any low-cut shirt, side boob exposed and ten feet of cleavage, it's perfectly normal and even embraced. I experienced this atrocious disgust as I sat down with my oldest daughter one Saturday afternoon at an outdoor mall. I chose a bench isolated from everyone so I could feed her. Since I was having a hard time with her latching, I always preferred to not be around too many people. That way, no one would see me struggle, which would compromise my confidence and screw it all up. Low and behold, out of the trenches came Cruella de Vil, walking with her husband, stick lodged way up her ass. She passed right by me and said, "I don't know why these women have to do that in public." All the blood boiled through every inch of my body. Mind you, she was in her late fifties, probably, so she is definitely someone who ought to be applauding a breastfeeding mother. I feel like older generations are the people who should be the most encouraging, but perhaps I am just crazy.

I called out after her, "Because my baby is hungry and that's what these boobs are for, lady! Maybe if someone would have breastfed you, you wouldn't be so miserable." I just needed to say that. Don't throw my book out. I actually don't think people who weren't breastfed are miserable assholes. Although, maybe a study could be conducted. Now, I am curious.

My tips on breastfeeding are extensive. I know it's fucking hard. I am not going to tell you it's some majestic experience where you sit on a rocking chair while forest animals gather at your feet. The first three weeks you are in the School of Hard Knocks. It's hard as hell. Those wearying weeks can be wicked and worse if you have no clue what you are doing and little desire to do it. There are moments you might envision ripping off a tiny baby's head. I can't say that thought passed my mind, but perhaps my memory is foggy. Surely I must have thought it at some point! Some people say they don't have milk without even really trying. Others are told to use a breast pump the whole time, and what you are actually doing if you do that is drying yourself out. Therefore, I am going to begin with the basics and work my way up to the actual feeding. If you didn't breastfeed but know someone who is expecting, perhaps these words will provoke new thoughts on the masochism that is this beautiful devotion. Do not hesitate to share information you may like or anything that makes sense to you. Just because you did not do it, doesn't mean you can't push it on someone else and watch them suffer.

Make the Decision Early

Decide if you are going to breastfeed or not while you are pregnant. I tell you this because breastfeeding is 90% mind and 10% milk. The first couple of weeks you should not mix formula with breast milk, as they are very different. It can cause colic. Maybe your baby has a stomach of steel that can handle whiskey, but you don't know that, do you? Formula is thicker and has added ingredients. Breast milk is pure and more water-based. If the baby is feeding from a bottle and doesn't drink all of the mixture of formula and breast milk, you have to throw out the leftovers. Bacteria will result from the baby's saliva. What a waste. You can store breast milk in the fridge for longer. You have twenty-four hours to consume formula. You have to become a damn milk expert on top of all your other duties, and whoever is helping you care for the baby does too. That way, you are all on the same lactation page and baby does not get ill. Also, you do not want to waste precious breast milk. That is the sin of all sins. Real pain is seeing your freshly pumped breast milk spill all over the place by mistake. This happened to me. I tipped over six ounces of my milk because I was tired and clumsy. Do cry over spilt breast milk. I did.

People can't get enough of asking the breastfeeding question to pregnant women, mandating a response, which is basically asking if you are going to be an asshole or not. "Jackie, are you going to use nature's milk or opt for the easy way out?"

Very quickly, you can be made to feel like a pile of shit for saying you're not going to breastfeed, feeling obligated to offer reasons or excuses. Truthfully, you don't have to feel one way or another. However you decide to feed your baby is your business. Still, let me remind you, breast milk is free milk. I don't know how much formula can cost in a year, but it's a lot more than free. If that isn't motivation in itself, nothing else will be. If you are one of these coupon aficionados who walks into the store with no intention of buying but then walks out with thirty-three detergents, twenty-eight dental flosses, and forty pasta sauces, you can understand how free milk around the clock is something to rejoice.

You Can Do It. Put Your Heart into It.

At about the third month of your either miserable or heavenly pregnancy, your extremely hormonal body begins to produce colostrum. Consider that liquid gold milk from the ancient Egyptian tombs. It is the introductory yellowish milk produced by the mammary glands, and it is exactly what the baby needs when she is born and for the first days. This milk contains vitamins, minerals, antibodies, fats, carbohydrates, proteins, and a lot of other shit descended from the Gods themselves. Whatever God, Gods, or Higher Beings you have integrated into your life, breast milk comes from their heavens.

I cannot stress enough to give your baby this milk for two weeks, at the very least. Perhaps you have heard that breast milk is "nature's vaccine." Believe every word of it. Allow your baby to drink what is rightfully theirs. Your body has been waiting for this its whole life and seldom fails. Plus, it's free. Free. Free. Costs zero dollars. A lactation specialist may cost you about $250, which is indisputably worth it if you are having complications and want to succeed. I had no idea these people existed when I attempted to breastfeed my first kid, also known as The Experiment. I had to figure it out on my own and I didn't even have peer advocates to lean on. At minimum, two feedings a day consisted of my daughter being the splitting image of Carrie drenched in blood on prom night. Her horrible latch would cause me to bleed all over her face, resulting in me ugly crying out of sheer frustration, not physical agony. It was a bloody mess, literally, and as traumatizing as it sounds, it went on for the first two months.

After the third month, the United States and my bank account forced me back to work. The stresses of my job caused my milk to begin drying out. I was giving her formula for the most part and only breastfeeding her twice a day. In my feeble attempts to pump at work, I ended up annoyed. Usually, I was interrupted and I read somewhere that if you are highly stressed, as I was both at home and at work, the milk you are producing is not as healthy anymore, something about the exchange of negative energies. Needless to say, one day I had enough. I began the process of ending my milk production altogether, and in doing so, I felt guilty and defeated. In spite of the aforementioned impediments, I'll always be damn proud that I gave it my best shot and that I force fed her the magic golden milk. I'm basically Hathor, the Goddess of Motherhood, but in soggy pants, a bun, and smeared winged eyeliner.

It's Teamwork!

The benefits outweigh the literal titty aches. I see it as something fundamental. It does not mean you have to see it that way. The beauty of bearing children is that we can do exactly what we choose to do, unapologetically. Most women get at least one month to be home with their new baby. The way I see it is, if you are home anyway, why not give it a whirl? If it isn't for you, then it isn't for you, but it's definitely "for" the baby in almost all situations. Breast milk is an immunity booster. It is the only way all other mammals can feed their young, but we humans have choices. I think that is what causes many of the failures in breastfeeding. The fact that it sucks combined with easy access to formula makes it almost forgivable, for lack of a better word.

I am not telling anyone what to do with their milk jugs. What I hope to reinforce are the reasons women should try to breastfeed and shed some light on fears, doubts, and even facts. I believe that when mothers become informed, they often dare to try new things, and if they don't try it because it's too late for them, they preach it to the next mom. Did you know that there is sufficient research that discloses that aside from the healthy start you offer your baby, you also lower your own chances of breast and ovarian cancer? As if that wasn't enough good news, you also lower your child's chances of breast and ovarian cancer, and the longer you do it, the better it works. Studies also show that breastfed babies are less likely to be obese. I am sure we are all aware that obesity is an epidemic that is not subsiding any time soon. I am not going to illustrate charts and pie graphs, but there is quite a lot of information on the matter and plenty of resources to lean on (e.g., breastcancer.org and medicalnewstoday.com).

What is most amazing to me about breast milk is that it builds antibodies, so if a mother gets sick, the milk automatically readjusts to build antibodies to protect the baby from catching the virus. I learned this when my second baby was born. Two months after she was born, I returned to teaching belly dancing two times a week at a school with grade school children. I caught strep throat three times, almost back to back. A woman's immune system after giving birth is weak. It was incredible to me that the baby didn't even get a booger. Upon researching why, I learned that breast milk builds antibodies to protect the baby from catching a bug! The best thing to do if you caught a cold, flu, or bug is to continue breastfeeding. The antibiotics I was prescribed still allowed me to feed her my milk. You can't say that isn't hair-raising information!

Through the years, I have also noted that women don't have the support they need during their breastfeeding journey. While there are numerous perks to it, this breastfeeding shit is hard, and it is even more strenuous when you don't have support. If your health has been jeopardized or you just cannot breastfeed but would like to, the next best thing to your own milk is the milk of other women who are producing sufficient milk to share the love. Wet nursing is an ancient practice and, indubitably, an option to consider. Physical causes—such as polycystic ovary syndrome, thyroid disorders, postpartum depression and mental disorders, insulin resistance, inverted nipples, just to name a handful—can be the culprits of low milk supply. They can also make breastfeeding impossible. If you cringed at the suggestion of human milk sharing, I hope you never drink the milk of any other animal in any form. The following are three organizations with support, information, and guides:

- The Lactation Foundation
- La Leche League International
- International Lactation Consultant Association

A 2017 article from the American Psychological Association explained that longer breastfeeding predicts increases in maternal sensitivity over time:

> Women who breastfeed their children longer exhibit longer maternal sensitivity well past the infant and toddler years, according to a 10-year longitudinal study. The result held even after accounting for maternal neuroticism, parental attitudes, ethnicity, mother's education and presence of a romantic partner. The findings are published in the journal *Developmental Psychology*.
>
> ...
>
> Maternal sensitivity was defined as the synchronous timing of a mother's responsiveness, her emotional tone, her flexibility in her behavior and her ability to read her child's cues.
>
> ...
>
> The researchers analyzed data from 1,272 families who participated in the National Institute of Child Health and Human Development's Study of Early Childcare.
>
> (Jennifer Weaver, "Bonding Benefits of Breastfeeding Extend Years Beyond Infancy", *American Psychological Association*, October 30, 2017)

There is nothing to replace the bond between a mother and her baby as they feed together, smothered in skin, warmth, and pure love. It's a feeling of complete ecstasy that only another breastfeeding mother can comprehend. In my humble opinion, all babies are deserving of this. It is what they come into this morbid world most yearning...human touch, their mother's vibrations, and care. Don't be an asshole. Whip your milky boobs out and put that baby on tap.

Martha and William Sears's *The Breastfeeding Book* states the following:

> Derrick and Patrice Jelliffee, pioneers in breastfeeding research stated that breastfed infants are "biochemically different." This difference in body chemistry may be the reason they are healthier. While babies are breastfeeding, they have fewer and less serious respiratory infections, less diarrhea, and less vomiting. When breastfed babies do become ill, they are less likely to become dehydrated and need hospitalization. (Martha Sears, RN and William Sears, MD, *The Breastfeeding Book*, 2017)

Random Tips Straight from My Bra

With my second baby, I was determined to succeed at this breastfeeding challenge because that is what it can be...a damn challenge. I knew that newborns need to eat every two to three hours, and they are not, in fact, supposed to sleep through the night. Newborns eat as much as the size of their fist, so do not worry that your milk is not enough because it is adequate for what their bodies can hold. They are just going to need it frequently. One day, I decided I was going to go to Babies "R" Us "real quick", and I took a little longer than three hours. That night, I woke up in a cold sweat, fever, chills, and a pain in my left breast that was unfathomable. I knew instantly I had mastitis. One of my fucking milk ducts was clogged because I wanted to shop for newborn pajamas. There is no Drano for that. I knew I had to keep feeding the baby because her sucking would unclog it, so imagine how fun that was. Mastitis is one of the reasons women give up. I get it! It is not pleasant. It's painful, annoying, and nerve-racking. I eventually phoned my midwife because the pain was excruciating, even for me, who has a high threshold for pain (and stupidity). I was told that if it proceeded past twenty-four hours to go to the doctor and get antibiotics that were okay to take while breastfeeding.

In a matter of just six months, I had gotten strep throat three times, a stomach bug, and mastitis, not in that order. Ladies, if I can get through that bullshit, so can you! My youngest daughter was breastfed for three and a half years. I never meant to go that far. It just happened! My goal was a year. Then it was two. Then, in the subsequent months, she enjoyed the bond and being a stay-at-home mom made it easy to do. Knowing that through every new stage of her growth my milk was producing new nutrients to aid in her development motivated me to continue. During that time, I'll have you know that my breast milk helped me time and time again! For sore, cracked nipples, apply some of your own breast milk! I didn't have contact solution one night and guess what? I used breast milk to soak my contacts in. Worked like a charm. Mosquito bite on my oldest also was treated with my milk. She got constipated a couple of times because she does not tolerate gluten very well. I gave her a spoonful of breast milk and she pooped like a champ. My fiancé enjoyed his coffee one day with a tad of breast milk and he still doesn't even know it. Since its doubtful he will read this, he shall remain oblivious to his delicious and super healthy morning cup of Joe.

Women, if you have a goal to breastfeed or you already are and are seeking to continue, I can offer you the following (unsolicited) advice: the best time to pump is right after the baby eats. Otherwise, using a pump regularly can dry your milk supply out. The first two weeks after birth, your brain is calibrating exactly what it needs to produce depending on how often your baby feeds from your boobs. The sucking sensation is different with a pump and confuses the brain, which is already overloaded trying to match all these outfits the baby wears three times a day. It is important to attempt to feed baby from you first and later introduce a bottle. Again, these are tips you don't want, but they may come in handy if you are ever in the predicament of ruining your life by getting pregnant. Keep some gel nipple pads handy. You can purchase them online, and I promise they will become your best friend. They are reusable cold pads for relief when your nipples are cracked and about to fall apart. This gets much better after the first month, once your inconsiderate baby learns to latch. While breastfeeding you even have to become scrupulous about what you eat since there are certain foods you may have to give up if your baby shows signs of an upset tummy. It can be something you are eating or drinking, and you must play the game of figuring out what it is. Oftentimes, it can be things like parsley, fish, caffeine, peanuts, garlic, dairy, or any other food or condiment you may be enjoying. Remember when I mentioned that babies are assholes?

The fourth trimester has a whole new set of mishaps, and sometimes I hear women say they wish they were still pregnant. The real nut jobs are the "I miss my belly" women. As for me, I'll take a month of mastitis over being pregnant. On the other masochist hand, I am one of the "nut jobs" who wistfully reminisces on the breastfeeding days and secretly wishes I could still prop my almost five-year-old on a boob and cuddle her. Go figure.

Although I am wearing my activism hat proudly, I recognize that breastfeeding isn't an option for everyone, and that is perfectly fine. As long as your baby is being fed, loved, and obsessed over, we are speaking the same language. Mothers have to support one another and celebrate our differences, too, but don't you forget how free this milk is.

"If you aren't yelling at your kids, you aren't spending enough time with them."

—Mark Buffalo

Chapter 10
When Is the Best Time to Have Kids?
(It's never, but read it anyway.)

Babies come with one purpose and one purpose only and that is to ruin you. It's literally never the precise time, in my humble and unbiased opinion, to make the plunging decision to start a family. Kids are family members you can't get rid of, no matter what they do. Remember that. You can't throw them out of the family tree like you can do to your alcoholic Aunt Marie who falls into the Christmas tree every Christmas Eve and sets the dog's hair on fire with her cigarettes. Kids are for keeps. I am not reluctant to tell you that if you decide to wait around for all the stars and planets to align with your mind, body, career, spirit, reproductive system, and so forth, you'll never bite the bullet. Unless you must plan your pregnancy because you need to seek an alternate option, such as a fertility center, almost all pregnancies are unplanned. I dare say most of the population was an "oops," and some more than others, if you know what I mean.

If you are a Virgo or a Capricorn and you need a blueprint for your entire existence or you'll need to be put on medication, then by all means, plan your childbearing years along with every other minute of your day. Be forewarned, regardless, that you'll still never be ready. Going from zero kids to one is a shit show. Going from one to another one is shit show part deux because you have to adjust to parenting two completely different beings. You're adding more to the parenting plate, dealing with a sibling who is possibly resenting the new baby and everything additional that goes with a growing family. It can be stressful for everyone. You'll be overwhelmed trying to find a routine to balance out the dynamics of your life those first few weeks. Surprise! There is no routine!

The Future Is Blurry

It's after the second kid that it doesn't matter anymore, from what I hear. Then, it's like, "Whatever, they will figure it out." The real conundrum comes when you are no longer in the family of four bracket and adding a third child means going headfirst into a minivan. It also means being omitted from family of four vacation packages. If you are dining at a restaurant, the booths and tables for four will not work for you either, and you'll be forced to wait for a bigger table, not to mention thrice the screaming, thrice the whining, and thrice the spending in all directions. As you can see, there are levels to this melodrama. When I see families who have four kids and more, many questions formulate in my mind. I want to investigate how they do it. How does that mother keep her shit even semi-together? Maybe they should be writing parenting books, but with what time? They are the ones who possibly possess the best, juiciest advice and solutions superior to the commonplace advice of feed your kids, make them shower, force them to eat their vegetables, don't let them play with knives, and teach them to say "please" and "thank you."

Seldom do you hear someone say they chose the perfect time to have kids. If you do hear it, fuck those people. This book is for everyone, but primarily for women who hated being pregnant, who took pregnancy tests in a Denny's bathroom as they crouched over a dirty toilet praying for a blue line and didn't necessarily plan on having kids when it happened, but look at you now all grown up and collecting fitted sheets. I had my first kid at thirty, for example, and when I was pushing out that baby, I had friends whose kids were graduating from middle school. Now, I am raising a toddler and a grade school kid, and I have friends who have kids about to start college. "The best time" depends on what way of life better suits you. I mean this in the sense that I was able to enjoy my youth and do all of the things, carefree, that young adults do in their twenties. However, at almost forty, when I am fucking tired,

I am experiencing full-blown Mom Life. On the other hand, acquaintances who started reproducing as early as nineteen years old are just about done with most of the boot camp parenting bullshit. They can go through their midlife crises in peace and take well-deserved breathers more often, while people like me are currently situated in front of multitudes of piles of laundry folding tiny socks, yelling, "Get that of your mouth!" six times a day. They gave up their youth, but freedom is on the horizon. For us late bloomers, the horizon is blurred and almost nonexistent and will remain so for a long, long time. Help.

Waiting…and Waiting

The bona fide "right time" is when you can admit you are ready to do a lot of waiting. Allow me to sketch out some situations for you. As a parent, you will have to wait for babies, toddlers, and kids to shit. You have no idea how big of an ordeal shitting is with kids. From the moment they are born you begin wiping and cleaning it. You become a scholar in the colors of the shit color spectrum, and you learn what to do if it's black or green, too hard or too soft. When the dreadful days of potty training start, hold on to your mom jeans because that is a hell of its own unique grandeur. Personally, it is my least favorite part of raising kids and I have a lot of least favorite parts, including some I know nothing about yet: the teen years.

Once they grasp the concept of using the potty, hopefully before age four, they still won't know how to wipe their butts, so you'll be a butt-wiping servant. You aren't a real parent until you have had to clean shit from under your nails. You pretty much have an untrained puppy on your hands whose whole house is a toilet. I have never had to deal with kids who decide to take off their dirty diapers, either inside the crib or just anywhere in the house, sending their poop flying in all directions and also smearing it wherever they please, but that is also something some babies do, like the little hell raisers they are.

You'll spend a considerable amount of time waiting on kids to eat their meals, find their shoes, put them on, do their homework, get dressed for school—things of that nature. You'll have to wait for them to explain something, which normally takes sixty seconds, in fragments while repeating the same thing an excruciating amount of times. You'll have to wait for tantrums to pass, fevers to subside, and odd phases to end, such as the slime phase. Slime everywhere! My household products don't stand a chance, as we are currently knee-deep in the slime phase. You'll be sitting in the waiting areas of urgent care centers, swimming pools, dance studios, soccer fields, and other places where you can't drink. Somehow, you'll draw the patience for these shenanigans out of a magical place you didn't even know existed. You may even find yourself being happy to do it because you love them. You love them more than you love your damn self. There is much truth to the responsible and pre-planned decision to wait until your career is in gear, you have the house of your dreams, or the three academic degrees you want, but again, this is all relative. I have seen young parents with nothing build a life while having kids. I have seen parents with multiple degrees raise kids in ways that, to my standards, are not exactly the best. I have also seen families with not much education raise amazing, respectful children, far from intolerable. I guess the right time is when you are ready to test the fortitude of your patience.

The End of Me Time

If you are currently enjoying your Me Time to the fullest, taking pleasure in spontaneous adventures, treating yourself to spa days or shopping sprees from time to time, know that these simple life joys will be more limited. For a greater chunk of the population, many sacrifices have to be made once kids join the equation. Not everyone can splurge freely because parental responsibilities and priorities weigh heavy. You'll find yourself at a store with multiple items and then end up leaving things you planned to get for yourself so that you can get things for your kids instead. It's a jarring change to have to be less selfish and think of yourself last, but it is a reality you must mentally prepare for when becoming a parent.

Some people don't even become real adults until they have children, and I am talking about myself here. I grew up at thirty, regardless of already being on my own and having a full-time job. It was not until I had a child that I truly had to make adult choices and lifestyle changes. I used to be able to get up and either do whatever I wanted or lazily stay in bed all day on a Sunday. I could plan a trip in a plane or on a cruise ship if I pleased and didn't have to worry about taking care of anyone. Those were the days! I know all moms have mental vacations where they regress to those days of being footloose and fancy-free. I don't care if you had kids at eighteen. You'll miss being six. Parenthood is about giving shit up and trading your peace and serenity for chaos and worry that never subsides, but we love it, don't we? Masochism is a hell of a drug.

Why Have Kids at All?

After your baby is born, you wait and anticipate every milestone approaching. It's like Christmas morning every time they surprise you with even the stupidest new movement. You just wait for the next cute move. You take about fifty pictures a day and share them with people who don't give a single shit about a new tooth or a first haircut, but it's always exciting to you. No matter how many kids you have, you wait for the milestones, and you celebrate them with new eyes. You eagerly and anxiously anticipate all the new stuff that unravels. Once they roll over, you can't wait for them to sit. When they sit, you can't wait for them to stand and walk and get jobs and stop asking you for money.

It's a waiting game, but time is a beast, and you have to take life pauses every now and again to soak it all in. Why have kids at all, you may ask? Well, I suppose so that you aren't alone in this world. You won't always be the young buck you see in the mirror. Have a kid so you have a nurse when you're old and useless. Then, you can remind them of all the things you had to endure when they were growing up. Pile on the guilt trip, and they have no choice but to take care of you forever. Have a kid to teach yourself how to not be so damn selfish and egocentric. Challenge your ego to love someone other than yourself for once. The more kids you have, the bigger the army to make sure you are wiped properly in your eighties. As a matter of fact, the only reason to have multiple kids, aside from the army of caregivers you need, is so they have each other when you're dead. Maybe they will all be super close.

Perhaps they'll hate one another, but they are still on the same planet, and they know they have siblings. Whatever your reasons are for embarking on the ludicrous ride that is parenting, the most important thing to know is that it's not a role to be taken lightly, as there will be an extreme change of axis in the universe you are familiar with. This is something you must throw your whole being into, no half-assing it. Kids are a pain in the ass, but they didn't ask to be born.

The right time to have children is when you are ready to give someone, who can't give you anything but kisses and high fives in return, your whole heart, much like in the video game *Mortal Kombat*, nothing more, nothing less.

Chapter 11
A Dose of Unsolicited Advice

Sheila: Oh my god, Linda. This lady in the parking lot of the farmer's market told me I'm not using my car seat properly. Who does she think she is? Rear-facing my baby until age two because she says it's safer sounds insane! Right?

Linda: Well, but she's actually right, Sheila. Extended rear-facing a toddler is safer. A toddler's spine is still highly delicate and, with a strong enough impact, could sever. Rear-facing is safer.

Sheila: But my son's legs are too long and they can break.

Linda: True, but it is better to have broken legs than a fractured vertebra.

Sheila: Whatever. Everyone has an opinion.

Sometimes, Sheila responds with, "You know, I had never heard of extended rear-facing. I'm going to look into that later." In that magical moment, a star is born.

The Most Important Advice in This Book

There will never be a shortage of recommendations from other parents, that's a given. However, I feel that this car seat advice I am placing on your conscious is possibly the most important. My hope is that if you have a child in any type of car seat—infant seat, booster, five-point harness, convertible car seat—your mind turns to the lady with a face mask who once soaked her contacts in breast milk.

I don't care where you live. Cars are dangerous places for us all. All we do is go on and on about how ruthless everyone is behind the wheel. According to the general consensus, no one knows how to drive. We just don't have control of what can go wrong from point A to point B, so why not do what is safest, once we know what that is? The problem lies in that we always think it cannot happen to us. We believe we are invincible until we find ourselves living in the nightmare we never saw as a possibility. I know I have one of the few kids going into the third grade in a booster seat, with back rest and everything. She was one of the few kids who rolled up into the first grade in a convertible car seat. I have been called ridiculous, many times by her. I don't doubt people who know me have called me the same in their minds or gossiped about me to their friends. That's okay. I'll be ridiculous my whole life if it means protecting my kids. Someday they might thank me, but I won't hold my breath. The car seats I have both girls in are for up to a hundred pounds. It's quite possible they will start high school sitting pretty right there. That's what we say at home, which is a big fat joke. Obviously, they're going to arrive at their weddings in the car seat because safety first and nutrition second. How many people weigh a hundred pounds on their wedding day? My mom did, actually, and she looked fabulous!

Car seat safety isn't a parenting style. It's a serious precaution we should try and learn more and more about so that we aren't on the news with smeared mascara talking about, "I don't know what happened." All car visors tell us plain and clear that backseats are the safest place for children, as if that wasn't common sense. Yet, people who have space in the backseat allow children under the age of twelve to ride shotgun. They sit their precious cargo directly in front of a gigantic piece of glass surrounded by air bags that can kill a child if they deploy. Granted, you may get lucky your whole life and never crash, but why take that chance? I encourage you to read the car seat safety laws in your state, but also research how you don't have to adhere to that. You can choose to do what is absolutely safest for the child you birthed while still abiding by the law.

Extended rear-facing (ERF) is a real thing. It's the better thing, as a matter of fact, and not opinion. I understand that at the twelve-month mark it is considered a milestone to turn the seat over, but that is not the safest option at that point. I once didn't know either. There is a small window of time in which you can harness your child into a seat and constrict much of their movement. Why are we not all on board with doing so for as long as possible?

A mom reached out to me on Facebook after I posted a cute picture my girl forward facing at a year and four months. She politely asked me if I knew what ERF was. When I said no, she sent me a bunch of information, including links to videos of crash test dummies that showed what happens to toddlers' car seats when there is an impact. Needless to say, I turned her seat around the very next day. I was grateful that she took the time to involve herself in my business and stick her nose in my car seat picture because it could have saved my daughter's life. Fortunately, nothing ever happened, but it could have. Nobody is going to mourn your child for an eternity like you. Numerous articles are now backing up ERF, but the best article I have found about Extended Rear Facing until the age of two is from Consumer Reports by Emily A. Thomas, Ph.D. It explains that children up to twenty-three months are 75 percent less likely to die or sustain serious injury in a rear-facing car seat than a forward-facing one. Three different car seats are recommended for kids throughout their childhood: rear facing infant carrier, a convertible, and a booster. I remember walking through the car seat aisle at Babies "R" Us a few years back and there were new posters suggesting that babies be kept in a rear-facing position, and that made me pretty happy. People may read it, think it over, and still choose to transition, but the information is out there to be received.

Quick Car Seat Tips

- Never put your child in a used car seat if you can avoid it. You don't know how used it is or if all of the parts are working correctly. Car seats expire, so if you must, look for the number that tells you when it becomes outdated.
- Use the chest clip as a chest clip, not at stomach level where it does nothing to protect the child. It should always remain at armpit level.
- You should not be able to pinch any slack on the straps. They ought to be snug but not too tight.
- Always remove winter coats and heavy jackets before strapping your baby/toddler/child in the car seat.

- Convertible car seats for up to a hundred pounds are out there, so put your big ass kid in one and drive with the peace of mind that they are in the safest situation.

Instilling Fear in Your Kids

For the most part, this is all unsolicited advice, which was given to me in a span of nine years and now I want to share it. I know it's baffling, but I always welcomed strangers' advice the same as I would friends' and family's advice. Like everyone else, I eventually did whatever the hell I wanted, but I consider much of what I am told from other mothers. A lot of it really comes from a good place. Other parts are just advice I pulled out of my own experiences, planting them on your lap and hoping for the best.

In this world where every other day you hear of kids being taken, hit by cars, or, worse, involved in child-trafficking, I live in constant and incessant fear of my children disappearing even for a second. I have tried my best to instill fear in them of what can happen if they leave my sight. I have a child who is the friendliest person on the planet. She navigates toward anyone and sparks up conversations, tells everyone her life story, and is so free-spirited that it's a sheer terror to me. There was one particular day I will never forget, and she didn't either for a while. We were at a science museum in Colorado. I was at the pinnacle of desperation with her running off, even a short distance, and I had already grown tired of repeating myself and explaining the dangers and consequences of her getting lost. I saw her wander off. I told my fiancé I was going to let her and, obviously, watch her very closely from behind. He was on board.

Just like I knew would happen, she began to look around and did not see us. There were walls made of rock and little nooks to hide in, where I was almost right behind her but could remain unseen. This little game of hide-and-seek that she didn't know we were playing went on for about two minutes, which must have felt like an eternity to her. She was afraid and started crying, so we approached her, and I had to forcefully explain that, just like that, she could get lost forever. This may seem harsh, but I had to do it. No one but me will be forever damaged if something happens to her. If someone gives you a dirty look, as I have gotten in a store for going bat-shit crazy at a kid who won't stay put, stare back and ask them if they are going to go help you find your child if she goes missing. The point is, protect those little shit stains to the best of your ability and with all of your might. Everyone will move on with their lives, eventually, but you won't, not completely, anyway.

My Worst Parent Moment

Pumpkin Patch Day in 2009 was a grandiose mess. It was my worst parenting moment by far. We stopped to get gas after pictures at the pumpkin patch, customary in the fall if you have kids. We were going to be driving about forty-five minutes, so I wanted to feed my daughter quickly in the backseat. I got out of the car, closed my door, and approached her door to get in. It was locked. I went around the car trying to open the other doors, and they were also locked. I panicked. I ran into the gas station to get the keys from her dad, and he told me I had them. No! I thought he had them. The car locked her in, and I didn't know what to do! She started crying. Someone realized what was happening and brought over a Slim Jim. He tried opening the car, but it wouldn't budge. In a matter of three or four minutes, I called the police and in another two minutes a police officer arrived. He had to break the passenger window so that we could open the door.

I can't begin to elaborate how god-awful that day was and how much mom guilt I carried with me for many months, leading into years. My advice here is pay attention! Make sure the doors of your car don't lock automatically. Equally, don't leave your kids in the car. This sounds silly, but these occurrences seem to be in the news frequently, and each time I have to read about a baby who died because she was forgotten in a car, my heart falls apart. My fiancé made the remark that maybe if people had to charge their phones on the car seats, they wouldn't forget their kids in the car. The reality of that statement is disheartening. Is this what we have come to? Are people so distracted they forget they have a baby in the backseat?

The Paradox of Motherhood

The paradox of motherhood is that women are expected to be birth goddesses, nurturing mothers to their new babies, and lose their pre-pregnancy weight in order to be stunning and sexy almost immediately. That hardly seems fair or right. You know what's sexy? A tired mother who is doing her best, whether it is her first baby or her sixth. Pregnancy, labor, and delivery make quite the cocktail of disaster on the human body. Recovery is important. Taking it easy is also important. The fourth trimester is about healing and trying damn hard to accept the body you have. All your weight loss issues and concerns can be dealt with in due time. A slow and patient recovery is your obligation. After you have a baby, your organs, bones, joints, hormones, and your entire skeleton is adjusting and readjusting. Everything is shifting back, and your vaginal muscles are reorganizing themselves. Consider yourself a small city rising up from an earthquake. If you choose to breastfeed, your uterus is contracting quicker and you are also burning about five hundred calories a day, which is always a bonus. Allowing your body and mind to revitalize is a favor you do for yourself. The first eight weeks should not be about any kind of weight loss, and if you are a human food truck, meaning nursing your baby, a diet ought to be the last thing on your mind. I realize we are living in times where the pressure is on to look a certain way, but the intelligent thing to do is to relax and give your baby that extra special attention she needs. Know that you have plenty of time to get back the body you had or the body you want.

Introducing Foods

Introduce foods you think your kids will hate early on, and this can equate to almost everything that isn't soaked in sugar. It's possible you'll have to reintroduce certain foods about ten times before they willingly eat it, much like I had to do with Brussels sprouts. One more day and I would have dipped them in Nutella and called it a day! In all seriousness, kids need to eat their damn vegetables, and that isn't a matter of opinion. No one is telling you to raise vegans or vegetarians, unless that is what you want, but greens and fruits should be an intricate part of everybody's diet.

Kids should not drink soda, and I know many do. Just know this is setting them up for terrible consequences, not limited to gum and teeth issues. Caffeine is addicting, and allowing children to incorporate sodas and an abundance of other sugars into their daily lives is leading them headfirst into unhealthy habits as they get older. My advice to any parent is to teach them the value of good foods so that as they grow, they will, more often than not, make better choices. I know this can be quite challenging because we want to see these brats happy and quiet. Allowing them to have the sweets they crave and beg for each and every time will get them to shut up for the time being, but don't forget what sugar does. It fills the void momentarily. After that, it gives false energy kids don't exactly need. Then, they become irritable, and lastly, they crash from the sugar rush. It's bad for their digestive and nervous systems as well.

Now, more than ever, there seems to be an influx of behavioral issues. Sadly, there are children who are sent to school with a belly full of sugar from either cereals or other breakfast foods high in sugar. Then, their teachers have to endure the effects of that accumulation of sugar, which are all of the aforementioned things—hyperactivity, irritability, and sluggishness.

Making healthier food choices can make a world of difference not only for alertness and behavior but also for maintaining a healthy immune system. Nothing is more potent than kid germs during flu season. They graciously pass the germs to adults who get it ten-fold! You'll hate your kid when he comes home with boogers and a cough he picked up from his schoolmates. You'll know in that instant that you are next. I'm not a doctor. These are mere observations I have made or concluded out of sheer common sense. In spite of all the amazing decisions we know we should be making for our kids, most moms know how easily dinner can be solved with pizza or mac and cheese. All hail the World's Okayest Mom choices as well because sometimes life takes you by storm. I don't believe there's a quintessential mom out there, so if your kids have had potato chips for breakfast one day or pizza for three meals in a day, we know that you're still doing your best. Start leaving pieces of broccoli between the couches so they have healthy surprise snacks to munch on.

Lies and Humility

Lying to your kid will become second nature. It is merely a means of survival as a parent and a way of enriching their childhood because without lying, you cannot effectively execute certain surprises. You'll lie about superficial shit like "beauty is skin deep", and then you'll lie about not having money for something when you really do. You'll lie about how you agree with some of their teachers on random complaints given to you when, in reality, you don't and you want to tell that crude, miserable teacher that teaching is not for her.

You'll lie and you'll lie, and my advice to you is: Don't ever feel guilty about it. Lying about mythical creatures like the Tooth Fairy is short-lived and brings upon stupid joy, for you and them. Speaking of the Tooth Fairy, I advise you to raise humble kids. I know we are living in the age of overdoing everything and showing off to people we don't even know, but I promise you that your $1, $2, and $5 will be embraced with as many "ooohs" and "ahhhs" as a higher, more ridiculous monetary amount. All you are doing is setting yourself up for disappointment later when and if you cannot deliver the same amount. Show your kids the value of being grateful for whatever they receive, which is hard today. Although I am not adhering to the exact blueprints my parents used in raising my brother and me, there are moments I do ask myself, "What would my parents have done in 1990?" I know we aren't in the 1980s or 1990s, and I have to "keep up with the times" or whatever, but you know what? Some things are timeless. Also, it is never too late to change the way you do things. I truly can't stress that enough.

Bedtime

I have been asked several times for advice on bedtime, which startles me and even makes me giggle. I find it amusing that people, bless their souls, would assume that I am doing something monumentally amazing during this dreadful time full of annoyances and problems. No one has more things on their agenda than a kid who has been summoned to bed. It's really enough to make you want to pull your hair out. No matter how many books you read to them or how many times you tuck them in and say goodnight, there is always one more glass of water to consume, ONE MORE TRIP TO THE TOILET! There will be some war every single night, guaranteed. This obviously escalates when there is more than one kid. It's a true test of your tenacity during these gut-wrenching hours known as "bedtime." It is the time most anticipated by parents, more so if you are a stay-at-home parent. My advice on bedtime is just yell a lot until everyone is crying, which they probably are going to be doing anyway, and then you may also want to resort to threats. Please see Chapter 2.

Advice on Gender

Try and focus your energy more on delivering a healthy baby than on what the gender will be because, guess what? Whichever sex you birth requires the same type of care. Both sexes are going to take you to the brink of despair and if you think it is easier to raise boys than girls, you need to recheck yourself and your surroundings. That's just one of the dumb things you hear through the parenting grapevine.

I distinctly recall someone once telling me something that resounded in my mind numerous times and at different situations, and now, I have the pleasure of sharing it with you. This woman said to me, and I quote, "I have my hands full with three kids, but at least they are all boys. Having girls is a lot harder, and there is so much more to worry about." When this message is first received, it might almost make sense, but if you have been paying any kind of attention to life right now, you quickly have to turn this down. I remember vaguely reminding her that whatever issues may arise with girls, boys will also face them. Boys have peer pressure, too. Maybe boys can't get pregnant, but they can impregnate and catch diseases from girls. They also have to be raised to respect themselves and everyone else. Boys can also be kidnapped, raped, and molested. That isn't exclusive to girls, and both sexes have to be raised to be fearless, confident, kind, and strong, while also knowing that it is okay to show emotion. These are tough times, and if you think that one sex is easier to raise than another, I hope you aren't shockingly surprised one day to learn that it is all the same cesspool of problems.

Perfect Your Poker Face

There will come moments in your parenting life when your kid will say something so ridiculous and out of left field that you will find yourself standing there bewildered, embarrassed, and helpless. There will be no one to save you from such abrupt craziness, and so I will not even advise you to prepare for such times. What I will tell you is that they will happen, and all you will be capable of doing is laughing, however inappropriate it may seem. That might be the only thing you can do—laugh and hope for the best. When my oldest daughter was three, we were at the park on a play date with a friend and her son. She decided to randomly run up to my friend and ask her why she was so fat. It was out nowhere, and I literally wanted the ground to swallow me. I did not laugh. I also understood that a three-year-old is not saying these things to purposely insult but rather as an observation. My friend laughed and noticed how utterly embarrassed I was. She reminded me that she was three and that it was okay. At age six, a different friend (thank goodness) came over with her new baby, only three months old. My daughter asked her if she had another baby inside of her and once again, I searched for the proverbial hole to crawl in.

So, you see, that is just one of the many unprecedented things that can occur when you least expect it, and the ground actually will not come to your rescue and swallow you. Other times, you will be in the comfort of your own home when suddenly you hear a ludicrous outburst. It could be something terrible and simultaneously comical they did, and you have to hold in your laughter because you are supposed to be angry and assertive. I have had to go into a closet so they don't see my face of sheer amusement. I dare say this is one of the more challenging parts of parenting—having to continue the role of being the adult disciplinarian while holding in an explosion of laughter because it isn't the time to let them in on how damn funny they are. Boss up, parents, and remain strong through these riveting times.

Will a Baby Make Your Relationship Stronger?

I am eager to share these words because I know in the deepest parts of my soul many people need to read this. A baby will either make you or break you, simple as that. If you are in a loving relationship, a baby will enhance that. If you are in a miserable relationship and you bring a baby into the world hoping this is the omen that is going to turn it all around, you are wrong. For the sake of minimal eye rolls and not being a Debbie Downer, I'll be bold enough to entertain the idea that it can go either way. I don't know any stories, personally, of how a baby fixed a relationship that was either on the brim of the toilet or already submerged. The possibility exists because miracles exist, but for the most part, a baby makes you or breaks you. A baby may be a temporary Band-Aid, but what is too far damaged cannot be mended by adding literally the most stressful thing on the planet to it—a kid.

Crayons Will Melt in Your Purse

Whenever I remember, I put crayons and paper in my purse if I know we are going to a restaurant. I have had crayons melt in my purse and markers pop in my bag, both annoying, but since I don't allow electronic devices at the table, I have to take some sort of prehistoric entertainment. I have little notebooks, mini Jenga games, and bullshit plastic toys. My advice is to do the same regardless of whether you allow tablets and smartphones because some of these restaurants only carry the cheapest of crayons. Your kids may want to use them. They will break in 2.5 seconds, and you'll be left with whiny kids and useless pieces of wax. It almost makes me want to demand that the managers of these establishments bring forth their income tax papers because I need to know why they cannot afford Crayola crayons! You're allowed to judge a family restaurant by what they provide kids to write with.

Do Parents Have Sex?

This is not a book about relationships, and I am no relationship expert, not by a long shot, but I have lent an ear to several friends and acquaintances who share a similar problem after having children and that is that their sex life came to a screeching halt. Obviously, I have made it clear that kids shit on everything sacred and important to you, and I think I have also made it somewhat excusable because their cuteness and artwork make up for it but not in the bedroom. They will get in the way of your libido and your overall sexy time if you let them. I have had people tell me that after a baby they no longer feel desirable, even though they are being desired by their other half.

Some people are so overwhelmed by the new baby that they forget how vitally important sex is in a relationship! This can be conflicting and confusing for both parties. It has to do with hormonal changes, additional stress that wasn't there before, changes in the physique, perhaps, and basically your brain being reprogrammed into the role of mother or father, and that is a big deal! Not everyone takes to these changes well. This does not mean it is a lost cause. It's necessary to be able to acknowledge each other's needs and concerns.

Taking care of a new baby or more than one kid leaves little time for self-actualization. It could be that time passes and one person in the relationship doesn't even notice that the romance has fizzled out. If there is a spurt where there is no sex or very little because of the accumulation of new responsibilities and a congested Diaper Genie, then you get past it. If you don't, you are basically roommates, and when there is trouble in the bedroom, there is trouble everywhere. I am inclined to also add that I believe a relationship can still flourish and thrive if one person cannot medically have intercourse because of a debilitating ailment and that isn't what a baby is, or is it?

Vacationing with Kids
A very direct piece of advice about vacationing with kids—do it every now and again, but just know those aren't vacations. Vacations are when you don't have to carry crayons in your purse or take a finger out of anyone's nose. The rest are family trips and in the words of Jerry Seinfeld, "There is no such thing as 'Family Fun.'"

Read to Your Kids
Make reading to your kids a habit, and even though there will be days you skip it, do make it a part of your lives. Read to babies, to toddlers, and to grade school children who can already read.

It's actually a simple pleasure that encourages cognitive development and allows for self-expression. Academically, it improves language skills, not to mention the beautiful emotional attachment from reading books dear to you and the kids. Allow them to relish in your sweet reading voice. A rather interesting article published in *The New York Times* states:

> It is a truism in child development that the very young learn through relationships and back-and-forth interactions, including the interactions that occur when parents read to their children. A new study provides evidence of just how sustained an impact reading and playing with young children can have, shaping their social and emotional development, in ways that go far beyond helping them learn language and early literacy skills. The parent-child-book moment has even the potential to help curb problem behaviors like aggression, hyperactivity, and difficulty with attention, a new study has found. (Perri Klass, MD, "Reading Aloud to Young Children Has Benefits for Behavior and Attention", *The New York Times*, April 16, 2018)

Makes me wonder if this works on adults too because it seems like we can all benefit from story time! For me, it's really fun, until one kid starts bickering over which book they want and it's obviously not the same book the other one wants and I have to take several deep breaths. Also, I enjoy listening to another type of voice coming out of me that isn't a crazy lady yelling. Bonus!

You Can't Spoil a Baby

People will be diligent in telling you how you should do things, from the moment you announce that you are pregnant, as I think I made clear. One aspect of parenting that I received a lot of the same advice on had to do with crying. First, I should proclaim that babies cry when they need something, as they are unable to self-soothe. I was advised to not hold the baby too much and to allow the baby to "cry it out" in a crib so she "learns" and doesn't get used to being picked up. This is, in my opinion, an evil sleep training method. It is common, though, and there are numerous articles and even books that teach the various methods. It wasn't until the baby was outside my body that I realized I was not the type of person who could parent this way. I also never understood how this teaches them anything other than they are being abandoned. I am attempting to tread lightly here because I know parents do this, but you don't have to. Babies do not understand what "spoiling" is. What they need is a warm, safe place like the one they had inside the womb. Consulting data from a research study, Anna Burbidge explains the following:

> The 1999 Ontario Early Years Study explains how the brain is being hard-wired in early development and how the patterns which emerge will last for a lifetime. How the adult brain reacts to stress is influenced by this early development, and adults who were stressed as babies can have abnormal stress reactions later in life, as well as greater vulnerability to social attachment disorders. (Anna Burbidge, "Letting Babies Cry—The Facts Behind the Studies", *La Leche League*, 2016)

After reading several articles about this and seeing that I was not crazy for wanting my baby near me all the time and never crying hysterically, I began to advise against crying it out, sharing with mothers that if they instinctively want to reach for their babies, they should! Imagine how awful it is to be crying in a dark room alone. What actually happens after a prolonged cry session? You get a headache. You feel tired and weak. I don't think this would be different for a baby, and they eventually will go to sleep, out of exhaustion. I don't think there is anything sadder than that. My advice is to trust your instincts. You don't have to do what your mother, aunt, best friend, or neighbor did with their baby.

This Last Piece of Advice Is Crucial

All moms strongly believe they are doing the very best they humanly can for their kids, making the adequate sacrifices, and making shit happen. That said, don't ever tell a stay-at-home mom that she doesn't do anything all day. Don't ever be crazy enough to even ask what it is she does all day because the answer is, she does everything. The End. Equally, don't ever tell a working mother that she doesn't spend enough time with her family. I can bet that woman is doing what she has to for her unappreciative kids, just as the stay-at-home mom is doing all she can for her unappreciative kids. Be careful what you say to a tired, frazzled, under- or over-caffeinated mother about how she mothers, especially if you do not have children of your own. You've been warned.

Chapter 12
Words of Encouragement and Discouragement

It's hard to remember a time that I wasn't sorting through toy boxes or cutting meat into tiny pieces, but I know those days existed because there are some wild pictures of me still up in lost files of MySpace. As strange as it still feels to not have the freedom I used to during those glorious days, it's safe to say, my days now, which are spent reading Olivia books on repeat, complaining about how dubious the common core grade school math is, and comparing brands of diaper rash cream, are much more fulfilling. That being said, it is quite the everlasting push and pull of yearning for the days you could shit in peace and concurrently loving the never-boring journey that is Parenthood. The allure of having kids is, well, there actually is none. You just find simple joys in day-to-day things. I mean, throughout your life you are sort of being prepared for the day you possibly reproduce. I'll explain how because you probably haven't taken notice. I know I hadn't.

Celebrations
Think of how many baby showers and kids' parties you were forced to attend when you didn't have kids. You had to give up your Saturday or Sunday, buy a gift for the celebratory kid and sit through hours of children yelling in bounce houses, crying during piñatas, and stepping on your clean shoes at parks. But, you showed face because it was your niece or nephew, best friend's brat, or your friend from work. Don't get me wrong, even after you have kids, these invitations will be tedious to attend and then it's even worse. You have to take all of the aforementioned steps—gift, time, and so on—and you now have to get every-

one dressed in cute outfits and dart them out the door on time. At this point, showing face matters more because you know deep down that unless you attend other people's parties, you can't expect the same people to come to yours. It shouldn't be that way, but that's the truth. What's more, when you attend parties with kids of your own, you have to exit the party with your tired, smelly kids in tow and deal with them during the festivities. Some of these parties will be merciful enough to provide adult beverages, but you can't count on that!

Aside from baby showers—the ancient practice of gathering your friends and family and forcing them to buy your unborn child a gift while participating in embarrassing games to amuse your fat ass—now there are additional obnoxious commemorations like half-birthdays and gender reveal parties. Depending on the type of person you are, this is good news or, as I refer to it, obnoxious news. My parents threw me a luau baby shower for my first child, with all the bells and whistles. About 150 people arrived in Hawaiian shirts and dresses ready to limbo. It was beautiful, bless their souls, but I didn't enjoy it. I was exhausted. I tried to cover up my pale–from-anemia complexion with a sunless tanning spray and it came out uneven. There were a million people, some of whom I didn't even recognize. I threw up the BBQ chicken in a bush, and I couldn't have any of the fun punch.

My second baby shower I arranged at my house with a few friends and family because no one cares about the second kid, much less any after that. I think my parents came by and gave me a high five. If you're into that type of thing, though, you now can celebrate your baby's half-birthday and even have him smash half a cake. If you're into forcing people to care about the gender of your unborn child, you can have a gender reveal party. There are many creative ways to do this, from what I see on social media, including releasing pink or blue balloons into the sky, depending on what the gender is, oblivious to the fact that animals might eat the rubber and die. Realistically, I don't think anyone cares the gender of your baby, and a handful of people are probably thinking that you should just be happy that the universe is allowing you to have a baby in the first place. Perhaps, hope for perfect health instead of a specific gender. I see these types of parties as insensitive and pointless celebrations, as people have to also take time out of their weekend so you can announce something that is meaningless in the grand scheme of parenthood. It could be that I'm just a pain in the ass. I think it's a far more ingenious idea to have a party to reveal whether you are going to vaccinate or not or if you're going to circumcise or not, and then set the tone for everyone to argue and judge your future parenting decisions.

Cross Your Legs and Laugh

Truth be told, I would have liked to have had a book like this when I became a mom, and it's not because it is my work. It would have been nice to have had friends who were also new moms so we could have hated our lives together. I don't think I have ever told anyone, but I felt somewhat isolated as a brand-new mom, and I've since learned that this is not strange or uncanny. I feel that it's important to have outlets, inspiring people, and like-minded parents in your circle, not only to share information but also to just be there. The first time I was able to laugh wholeheartedly at this whole parenting thing was when I watched Louis C.K.'s stand up on his life as a dad. I recall my daughter was only one, and while his daughters were already a bit older, I was able to visualize all of those mishaps so clearly. I always knew deep down that motherhood would be a shit show, but when I heard him mock it so effortlessly, I knew it was going to be super amusing. Louis C.K. came to the Fillmore Amphitheater in Miami in December of 2010, and I took my dad so he could laugh even louder, which he did. I confess that I even peed a little, not surprising since my bladder was a hot mess still a year after I pushed my daughter out. Fast forward to eight years later, another kid, and about forty combined hours of pushing, my bladder is far worse. It's impossible to sneeze, cough or engage in robust laughter without having to cross my legs. I suppose I haven't been doing my Kegels.

I hope the next time you come across a noncommittal phrase like, "Motherhood can be stressful," you refer back to the pages of this book and instantly translate that to,

"Motherhood is RANCID. Motherhood is Hell, and Parenthood is comparable to a person from the 1800s being handed an iPhone and asked to send a text, make a phone call and take a selfie." For years, I have been listening to parents, mostly women, speak on behalf of their own experiences raising kids, and I felt compelled to portray this lunacy that is parenting in my own light. Whether it's listening to jovial advice like, "the hair dryer makes baby sleepy" (it does because it's white noise), or more grave topics like, can a flu vaccine be fatal? (yes, it can), the concerns, decisions, and reasons to worry as parents will be present, always, but so will the many opportunities to laugh, rejoice, and be grateful. The only (legal) things that are going to get us through the days, besides wine and chocolate are your peers who are in the same struggle, stepping in the same fucking slime puddles, and crying over similar Valentine's Day and Mother's Day cards.

As much as you may be dreading that play date, you never know who you will meet. That mom who doesn't seem to have anything in common with you could end up being one of your lifelong friends, and I have proven this to be true in my own life. As standoffish as I can be, I have spontaneously collided with women I never thought I would learn from or even lean on. The completion of this book, in itself, was made a billion times more special because I had the support of women who were eager to pre-order it, without even knowing if they would like it. How amazing is that? Women who have not had children yet, or have decided not to, pre-ordered my book to show support for everything they knew this meant to me. I cried a couple of times as I let it sink in that people were genuinely excited to receive a copy of my book. I am sharing this because I have been asked how was I able to complete it while being a stay-at-home mom of two. I know, I know, us stay-at-home moms just watch *The Wendy Williams Show* all day and get manicures. Well, it was a challenge, obviously, but it was not impossible, and I encourage any parent who doesn't feel they have time to pursue their dream to never give it up. It took me over two years. I actually watch almost no television, so instead of TV time, I make time for writing and reading books. I wrote on the toilet. I prolonged showers, while my girls were being supervised, and sat on the bathroom floor writing. I wrote in line at the grocery store, late at night, and whenever my parents and fiancé were generous enough to take the kids off my hands so I could gather some thoughts. Children will deplete your energy and kill your lust for life if you let them. Show those brats you can do it all because someday, sooner than you think, you will be encouraging them to pursue their dream, and wouldn't it be awesome to have something to show them, too?

If you made it to the grand finale of this book, I love you and thank you.

Dysfunctional Parent Checklist

___ You have used a towel to cover up pee on your bed and kept on sleeping.

___ You have burned bread or waffles, served it good side up, and hoped for the best.

___ You picked up food from the floor, wiped it, and gave it to your kid. Long live the five-to-ten second rule.

___ Pizza has been approved for breakfast on more than one occasion.

___ You showed up to a kids' party or baby shower on the wrong day.

___ You have forgotten at least one important event at your child's school.

___ You faked being sick to get out of a play date.

___ You've had wine for dinner.

___ You have faked a headache or a debilitating ailment to get out of playing with your child or helping her with something.

___ You can relate to more than one mom from the movie *Bad Moms*.

___ You forgot to wash school uniforms and sent the kids to school in regular clothes.

___ You have driven with an almost empty tank of gas with a kid in the car.

___ You have allowed bath time to be three times what it normally is just to have some alone time.

___ A handful of your child's artwork has been thrown in the garbage.

___ You've had to check your bank account in line at the grocery store.

___ You helped your kid look for a candy or chocolate bar you ate.

___ You let the kids stay up really late in hopes that they would sleep in the next morning.

___ You regifted your child a gift.

If you haven't gotten around to checking off each one of these, don't despair. I have faith in your dysfunction as a parent, and I don't doubt that you'll someday be able to check each of these off more than once.

About the Author

Jennifer De Paz is a stay-at-home mom who started her motherhood journey in 2009. The details of her life before that don't seem particularly important enough to mention because life begins when you have kids, right? She hopes to shatter your perception of whatever fantasy you have envisioned of parenthood and break through the false scenarios in diaper commercials. If you are already a parent, you will be able to relate with the trials and tribulations in all their raw glory. Jennifer encourages you to hide behind these pages as you ignore your child's soccer game. Breathe a sigh of relief in the realization that we all take mental vacations to the long lost days of freedom, the kid-free days. She finds fun in the irony that in spite of how knee-deep you may be in LEGO parts, play dates, and homework, you watch in adoration as your exhausting children sleep. You also can't help but talk about them to just about anyone who will listen. All parents are serving a life sentence, one we brought upon ourselves, although we'd like to imagine it ends when the kids turn eighteen. We can disagree on parenting styles, but we all share much the same worries and celebrate many of the same milestones and accomplishments. Jennifer can assure you that even she, who worked most of her life around other people's children, could have never been remotely prepared for motherhood. It's not a secret that no matter how much you may strive for perfection, you're still going to be a mediocre parent whose kids end up traumatized in some way.

Jennifer delights in hobbies like photography, vintage fashion, and long walks in arts and crafts stores. Her children are the culprits for her seemingly rapid aging, so a lot of makeup was used for this headshot. Jennifer lives in Miami, Florida, with her fiancé, two kids, two cats, and a toddler dog that might as well be a human. She is also wondering if anyone has seen her keys.